W9-AHY-582

WORLD BOOK'S
CELEBRATIONS AND RITUALS AROUND THE WORLD

World Book, Inc.

a Scott Fetzer Company

Chicago

This edition published in the United States of America
by World Book, Inc., Chicago.
WORLD BOOK and the GLOBE DEVICE
are registered trademarks or trademarks of World Book, Inc.

World Book, Inc.
233 North Michigan Avenue,
Chicago, IL 60601 U.S.A.

For information about other World Book publications,
visit our Web site http://www.worldbook.com, or
call 1-800-WORLDBK (967-5325).
For information about sales to schools and libraries, call:
1-800-975-3250 (United States); 1-800-837-5365 (Canada).

Copyright © 2003, McRae Books Srl
Borgo Santa Croce 8—Florence, Italy.
info@mcraebooks.com

All rights reserved. No part of this publication may be
reproduced, stored in a retrieval system, or transmitted in any
form or by any means electronic, mechanical, photocopying,
recording or otherwise, without the prior written permission of
the copyright owner.

ISBN: 0-7166-5017-7

McRae Books:
Publishers: Anne McRae and Marco Nardi
Series Editor: Loredana Agosta
Graphic Design: Marco Nardi
Layout: Sebastiano Ranchetti

Color Separations: Litocolor, Florence (Italy)

World Book:
Editorial: Maureen Liebenson, Sharon Nowakowski
Research: Paul Kobasa, Cheryl Graham
Text Processing: Curley Hunter, Gwendolyn Johnson
Proofreading: Anne Dillon
Indexing: David Pofelski

Printed and bound in Hong Kong by C&C Offset

1 2 3 4 5 6 7 8 9 10 09 08 07 06 05 04 03

CUMULATIVE GLOSSARY AND INDEX

Cumulative Glossary and Index

Table of Contents

Resources

Resources

Here is a sampling of other resources to look for at your school or public library. These resources on celebrations and rituals around the world are broken down into two groups: **General** resources and resources about **Specific Holidays or Specific Countries' Holidays.** Check with a librarian for suggestions of other resources.

GENERAL

Ancient and Annual Customs
by Dwayne Pickels (Chelsea House, 1998)

This book describes ancient customs and traditions that are no longer followed and provides the historic background of some traditions that are still enjoyed.

Anniversaries and Holidays
by Bernard Trawicky (American Library Assoc., 2000)

This reference source has more than 3,500 listings for U.S. and European holidays.

Celebrate!
(World Book, 2000)

Through lively text and colorful images, students learn how people celebrate all over the world and discover that every month of the year there is a celebration somewhere in the world. Students also can look up their birthdays in this volume to find out what famous historical figures were born on the same date. A glossary, resource list, and index are provided. This book is volume 14 of World Book's Childcraft—The How and Why Library set.

Celebrate: Four Seasons of Holiday Fun
by Brooks Whitney (Pleasant Company, 1998)

This book includes instructions for making holiday crafts and decorations, as well as directions for playing games and recipes for foods to celebrate different holidays throughout the year.

Chase's Calendar of Events
(Contemporary Books, 2003)

This annual publication is an indexed directory to special days and events of the year, including historical anniversaries, astronomical phenomena, worldwide festivals, celebrity birthdays, and culinary celebrations.

Children Just Like Me: Celebrations!
by Barnabas and Anabel Kindersley (DK Publishing, 1995)

Children around the world talk about and show their celebration customs and traditional costumes in this beautiful, brightly illustrated book.

Christian Festival Tales
by Saviour Pirotta (Raintree Steck-Vaughn, 2001)

Eight short stories about such major Christian holidays as Easter, Pentecost, and Christmas are included in this volume.

Coming of Age
by Lisa Sita (Blackbirch Press, 1999)

This title from the World Celebrations and Ceremonies series describes initiation rites and coming-of-age ceremonies from 10 countries around the world.

Coming of Age: Traditions and Rituals Around the World
by Karen Liptak (Millbrook Press, 1994)

Circumcision, body piercing, isolation, and ritual cleaning are only some of the puberty and coming-of-age rites of various cultures that are explained in this book.

DK Readers: Holiday! Celebration Days Around the World
by Deborah Chancellor (DK Publishing, 2000)

Special celebrations from around the world are described, giving their history and traditions.

Festivals

by Margaret Hall (Heinemann Library, 2002)

This book explores the history, food, music, and dance of different seasonal and religious festivals around the world.

Festivals and Holidays

(Macmillan Library Reference USA, 1999)

This reference volume contains descriptive information for more than 100 holidays, rituals, feast days, observances, festivals, and fairs celebrated around the world.

Festivals of the World

by Elizabeth Breuilly (Checkmark Books, 2002)

Breuilly provides the religious or historical background for a variety of festivals celebrated around the world.

The Folklore of World Holidays

by Robert Griffin and Ann Shurgin (Gale Research, 1999)

Arranged chronologically, this reference volume contains information about the folklore associated with more than 375 holidays and festivals celebrated in countries around the world.

Growing Up: From Child to Adult

by Anita Ganeri (P. Bedrick, 1998)

Simply presented and with colorful photos and drawings, the rites and rituals surrounding the passage from child to adult in the six major religions of the world (Hinduism, Buddhism, Sikhism, Judaism, Christianity, and Islam) are described.

Holiday Cooking Around the World

by Diane Wolfe (Lerner Publishing Group, 2001)

This title in the Easy Menu Ethnic Cookbook series is a collection of holiday recipes from 15 different countries.

Holiday Symbols

by Sue Ellen Thompson (Omnigraphics, 2000)

This guide to hundreds of symbols associated with 224 popular holidays from around the world covers foods, places, people, legends, and other aspects of the holidays.

Holidays Around the World for K – 12

a Web site at http://falcon.jmu.edu/~ramseyil/holidays.htm

This bibliography of Web sites will link you to information on specific countries and their holidays.

Holidays, Festivals, and Celebrations of the World Dictionary

edited by Helene Henderson (Omnigraphics, 1997)

This is a reference guide to popular, ethnic, religious, national, and ancient holidays, festivals, celebrations, commemorations, holy days, feasts, and much more.

How I Celebrate: A Young Person's Guide to Celebrations Around the World

by Pam Robson and Alan Brown (Millbrook Press, 2001)

Birth customs and ceremonies, coming-of-age rituals, wedding ceremonies, religious and historical holidays, and many other special rites of the Hindu, Muslim, Jewish, Buddhist, Sikh, Shinto, and Christian traditions are included in this book, which also contains appropriate recipes and crafts.

International Holidays: 204 Countries from 1994 through 2015: with Tabular Appendices of Religious Holidays, 1900-2100

by Robert Weaver (McFarland, 1995)

This reference book gives the reader the ability to identify the date on which a religious or secular holiday in 204 countries will be—or was—observed between the years 1994 and 2015.

Junior Worldmark Encyclopedia of World Holidays

by Ann Shurgin (Gale Group, 2000)

Approximately 30 holidays, festivals, and national and cultural celebrations in different countries around the world are included in this four-volume set that provides information on customs, traditions, ceremonies, folklore, clothing, food, arts and crafts, games, music, and dance.

Kids Around the World Celebrate!: The Best Feasts and Festivals from Many Lands

by Lynda Jones (John Wiley and Sons, 1999)

This book is a collection of recipes and hands-on activities that will give young people a taste of what it is like to be a part of a feast or ceremony in another country.

Kids Draw Funny and Spooky Holiday Characters

by Christopher Hart (Watson-Guptill, 2001)

Step-by-step directions are given for drawing a variety of characters associated with holidays celebrated in the United States.

Resources

Let's Celebrate Today: Calendars, Events, and Holidays
by Diana F. Marks (Teacher Ideas Press, 1998)

This chronological listing of holidays and multicultural events from around the world for each day of the year includes historical happenings, birthdays, famous firsts, inventions, and more. There are also three activities based on significant events for each day.

Let's Party!: Celebrate with Children All Around the World!
by Mick Manning and Brita Granstrom (Sterling Press, 2001)

Thirteen holidays from around the world are included in this book, which describes the costumes, food, games, and music that are part of these celebrations.

Multicultural Projects Index: Things to Make and Do to Celebrate Festivals, Cultures, and Holidays Around the World
by Mary Anne Pilger (Libraries Unlimited, 2001)

This reference book indexes more than 15,000 projects relating to multicultural handicrafts, foods, games, and activities that can be found in over 1,100 books.

New Year's to Kwanzaa: Original Stories of Celebration
by Kendall Haven (Fulcrum Publishing, 1999)

This collection of 36 original stories of religious and cultural celebrations from around the world includes historical events, myths, and legends.

Tales of Holidays
by Pleasant DeSpain (August House, 2002)

Nine short holiday folk tales feature stories from Russia, France, the United States, and other places.

World Holidays: A Watts Guide for Children
by Heather Moehn (Scholastic Library, 2000)

This illustrated alphabetical guide includes more than 100 religious, cultural, and national holidays celebrated around the world.

SPECIFIC HOLIDAYS OR SPECIFIC COUNTRIES' HOLIDAYS

All About Passover
by Judyth Groner (Kar-Ben Copies, 2000)

In addition to retelling the story of Passover and explaining the traditions of the Passover Seder, this book also includes recipes of traditional foods eaten during this celebration.

American Holidays and Special Days
by George and Virginia Schaun (Maryland Historical Press, 2002)

This book provides information on several religious and secular holidays, as well as other days that commemorate special occasions throughout the year.

Argentina
by Arlene Furlong (G. Stevens, 1999)

This indexed volume describes some of Argentina's many festivals, including the National Gaucho Festival, Carnival, and the National Immigrant Festival.

Asian Holidays
by Faith Winchester (Bridgestone Books, 1996)

Eight festivals celebrated by the Chinese, Japanese, and Vietnamese are included in this volume from the Read-and-Discover Ethnic Holidays series.

Australia Day – A History
A Web site at
http://www.australiaday.com.au/education.html

This Web site provides detailed information about how this national holiday is celebrated in Australia on January 26.

Autumn Equinox: Celebrating the Harvest

by Ellen B. Jackson (Millbrook Press, 2000)

This book tells about the significance of some harvest festivals around the world and about how these festivals are celebrated.

Birthdays Around the World

by Mary D. Lankford (William Morrow and Company, 2000)

Birthday customs, foods, and games from several countries, including Finland, Malaysia, Mexico, and New Zealand, are included in this book.

Brazil

by Marianna Serra (Raintree Steck-Vaughn, 2000)

This book discusses some of the foods enjoyed in Brazil and describes special foods that are part of their specific celebrations, such as Carnaval and the Bamba Bull festival.

Canada Day

by Patricia Murphy (Children's Press, 2002)

In simple style, the history, importance, and celebration of Canada Day are explained.

The Caribbean

by Linda Illsley (Raintree Steck-Vaughn, 1999)

The author describes special foods that are part of some of the Caribbean region's celebrations, such as Christmas and New Year, Carnival, the Crop Over harvest festival, and Phagwa.

Carnival

by Catherine Chambers (Raintree Steck-Vaughn, 1998)

This book introduces the holiday of Carnival and explains how it is celebrated throughout the world.

Celebrating a Quinceañera: A Latina's 15th Birthday Celebration

by Diane Hoyt-Goldsmith (Holiday House, 2002)

The customs and traditions connected with celebration of a Mexican American girl's coming-of-age birthday are described in this book.

Celebrating Passover

by Diane Hoyt-Goldsmith (Holiday House, 2000)

Through one family's celebration of Passover, the author describes the religious significance, traditions, customs, and symbols of this Jewish holiday.

Celebrating Ramadan

by Diane Hoyt-Goldsmith (Holiday House, 2002)

Following an American Muslim family throughout the holy month of Ramadan, the traditions, beliefs, and religious practices are explained.

China

by Amy Shui (Raintree Steck-Vaughn, 1999)

This book describes some of the special foods that are part of the celebrations of the Chinese New Year, the Tombsweeping Festival, and the Dragon-boat Festival.

Chinese New Year

by David Marx (Children's Press, 2002)

This simple introduction to the traditions and festivals of Chinese New Year is part of the Rookie Read-About Holiday series.

Christmas Around the World series

(World Book, various dates)

Each 80-page, beautifully illustrated Christmas Around the World book includes narratives explaining the common and rare customs of the region. Native Christmas songs, recipes, and crafts are also provided with detailed illustrations.

Christmas Presents Kids Can Make

by Kathy Ross (Millbrook, 2001)

Step-by-step directions are given for 29 gifts children can make from readily available materials for their family or friends.

Cinco de Mayo

by Lola M. Schaefer (Pebble Books, 2001)

This book offers a simple introduction to this holiday celebrated in Mexico each May 5.

Resources

Cinco de Mayo: Yesterday and Today

by Maria Cristina Urrutia (Groundwood Books, 2002)

Illustrated with historic lithographs and contemporary photographs, this book provides information about the holiday that commemorates Mexico's victory over France on May 5, 1862.

El Día de los Muertos

by Mary Dodson Wade (Children's Press, 2002)

This book explains how on November 1 Mexican families celebrate the lives of their deceased loved ones.

Divali

by Dilip Kadodwala (Raintree Steck-Vaughn, 1998)

Part of the A World of Holidays series, this book introduces the customs and practices of Divali as celebrated by Hindus around the world.

The Dragon New Year: A Chinese Legend

by David Bouchard (Peachtree, 1999)

Based on Chinese history and folklore, this is the story of a young girl who takes comfort in her grandmother's soothing story of a dragon, a mother's sorrow, and Buddha.

Festivals of the World series

(Gareth Stevens, 1997)

Each of the 45 illustrated volumes of this series covers a different country, introduces the reader to the festivals and cultures of the country, and includes crafts and recipes.

Fiestas: A Year of Latin American Songs of Celebration translated by Jose-Luis Orozco

(Dutton Children's Books, 2002)

Twenty Latin American holiday songs are featured in this beautifully illustrated bilingual book.

Hanukkah

by Jennifer Gillis (Heinemann Library, 2002)

The book presents a simple introduction to the symbols, celebrations, and traditions of Hanukkah.

A Hanukkah Holiday Cookbook

by Emily Raabe (PowerKids Press, 2002)

This is an informative book about Hanukkah that explains some of this holiday's symbols, ceremonies, and traditional recipes.

Happening Hanukkah: Creative Ways to Celebrate

by Debra Zakarin (Grosset & Dunlap, 2002)

This book is full of ideas for things one can make for Hanukkah or adapt for another occasion.

Hindu Festival Tales

by Kerena Marchant (Raintree Steck-Vaughn, 2001)

Stories, poems, plays, songs, and recipes make up this attractively illustrated book about four Hindu religious festivals.

Holidays and Festivals in Taiwan

a Web site at

http://www.gio.gov.tw/info/festival_c/index_e.htm

This Web site provides information on Taiwan's holidays that are associated with both the lunar and the western calendars.

Holidays for Children

Video series available on VHS and DVD (Schlessinger Media, various dates)

Twenty-two 25-minute videos give the origin and history of important holidays from various traditions around the world. Included in the series are: Arbor Day, Chinese New Year, Christmas, Cinco de Mayo, Easter, Election Day, Halloween, Hanukkah/Passover, Independence Day, Kwanzaa, Pow Wow, Ramadan, Rosh Hashanah/Yom Kippur, St. Patrick's Day, Thanksgiving, Valentine's Day, Remembering September 11th, Memorial Day/Veterans Day, Christmas Around the World, Groundhog Day, Martin Luther King, Jr. Day, and Presidents' Day.

Id ul-Fitr

by Kerena Marchant (Millbrook Press, 1998)

This introductory book looks at some of the ways Muslims around the world celebrate the joyous festival of Id ul-Fitr ('Id al-Fitr).

Indonesian Holidays
a Web site at http://www.expat.or.id/info/holidays.html

This Web site lists and discusses the four types of holidays that are celebrated in Indonesia: religious, national, international, and commemorative.

Islam
by Sue Penney (Heinemann Library, 2000)

This overview of the beliefs and customs of Islam includes an introduction to important holidays and worship practices around the world.

Italian Foods and Culture
by Jennifer Ferro (Rourke Press, 1999)

This book, which includes recipes, discusses some of the foods enjoyed in Italy that are part of the celebrations of St. Joseph's Day, Christmas, and the festival of Santa Rosalia.

Jewish Festival Tales
by Saviour Pirotta (Raintree Steck-Vaughn, 2001)

A collection of stories, poems, plays, and songs, this book includes six traditional stories concerning Hanukkah, Purim, and other Jewish holidays.

Jewish Foods and Culture
by Jennifer Ferro (Rourke Press, 1999)

Recipes for some of the special foods that are part of Bar and Bat Mitzvahs, Passover, and Purim are included in this book.

Judaism
by Sue Penney (Heinemann Library, 2000)

Important Jewish festivals and occasions, such as Rosh Ha-Shanah, Yom Kippur, Pesah, Sukkot, Shavuot, Purim, Hannukah, Bar and Bat Mitzvah, marriage, and death, are included in this volume.

Juneteenth!: Celebrating Freedom in Texas
by Anna Pearl Barrett (Eakin Press, 1999)

An African American family on a small Southeast Texas farm in 1945 prepares to celebrate Juneteenth, a June 19 holiday that honors the day General Granger arrived in Galveston with the news that the slaves had been freed.

Kwanzaa
by Amy Robin Jones (Child's World, 2001)

This book is an introduction to the seven-day African American holiday that has been celebrated since 1966.

Labor Day
by Carmen Bredeson (Children's Press, 2001)

This introductory work explains the origins of Labor Day and how it is celebrated.

Let's Celebrate Presidents' Day
by Peter and Connie Roop (Millbrook Press, 2001)

Information about the Presidents' Day celebration is provided in this book, including profiles of George Washington and Abraham Lincoln, the two men the holiday specifically honors.

Let's Celebrate Thanksgiving
by Peter Roop and Gwen Connelly (Millbrook Press, 1999)

This book includes information about the history of Thanksgiving, a craft activity, and a look at other harvest celebrations around the world.

Make Your Own Christmas Ornaments
by Ginger Johnson (Williamson, 2002)

This book includes 25 craft projects that can be made from readily available materials.

Martin Luther King, Jr. Day
by Dana Meachen Rau (Children's Press, 2001)

This book describes the history of Martin Luther King, Jr., Day and looks at some of the ways in which it is celebrated.

Martin Luther King, Jr. Day: Honoring a Man of Peace
by Carol Gnojewski (Enslow, 2002)

The author of this book presents the history and meaning behind the observance of Martin Luther King, Jr., Day.

Resources

Medieval Celebrations: How to Plan Holidays, Weddings, and Reenactments with Recipes, Costumes, Decorations, Songs, Dances, and Games

by Daniel Diehl and Mark Donnelly
(Stackpole Books, 2001)

In this book, you will find ideas and instructions for hosting a medieval feast to celebrate holidays, weddings, and other occasions.

Merry Things to Make: Christmas Fun and Crafts

by Diane Cherkerzian and Colleen Van Blaricom (Bell Books, 1999)

Step-by-step instructions are given for making a variety of simple handicraft items for the Christmas season.

Muslim Festival Tales

by Kerena Marchant (Raintree Steck-Vaughn, 2001)

Stories, a song, a poem, a play, a prayer, and a recipe provide insight into various Muslim festivals.

New Beginnings: Celebrating Birth

by Anita Ganeri (P. Bedrick, 1998)

This indexed volume introduces the rites and rituals surrounding the birth of a child in each of the six major religions of the world.

Night Lights: A Sukkot Story

by Barbara Diamond Goldin (UAHC Press, 2002)

Through this simple picture book, the festival of Sukkot is explained.

Las Posadas: An Hispanic Christmas Celebration

by Diane Hoyt-Goldsmith (Holiday House, 1999)

This photo-essay follows an Hispanic American family in a small New Mexican community as they prepare for and celebrate the nine-day religious festival that occurs just before Christmas.

Powwow

by George Ancona (Harcourt Brace, 1993)

Focusing on the Crow Fair in Montana, this photo-essay explains the preparations, participants, and festivities of the Native American festival called the powwow.

Presidents' Day

by Amy Margaret (PowerKids Press, 2002)

This book describes the history of Presidents' Day, the lives of George Washington and Abraham Lincoln and the monuments honoring them, and the ways of celebrating the holiday.

Public Holidays

a Web site at http://www.eastlondonsa.com/ddcal/public.html

This Web site lists the public, school, and religious holidays and the special days of selected African countries and gives the history of lesser-known ones.

Ramadan

by David Marx (Children's Press, 2002)

Marx gives a simple introduction to the traditions and festivities of the Muslim holiday.

St. Patrick's Day

by Amy Margaret (PowerKids Press, 2002)

This overview of the Irish holiday celebrated in both America and Ireland describes its history, symbols, special foods, and traditions.

Saudi Arabia

by Maria O'Shea (G. Stevens, 1999)

The culture of Saudi Arabia is reflected in its many festivals, including those described in this book: 'Id al-Fitr, 'Id al-Adha, and the Jinadriyah National Festival.

The Spring Equinox: Celebrating the Greening of the Earth

by Ellen Jackson (Millbrook Press, 2002)

Pictures and text describe how the arrival of spring has been celebrated throughout history.

The Story of Valentine's Day
by Clyde Bulla (HarperCollins, 1999)

In addition to including directions for making a paper valentine and sugar cookies, this book gives the history and customs of Valentine's Day from its beginning in Roman times to the present.

Switzerland
by Susan McKay (Gareth Stevens, 1999)

The Children's Festival, the William Tell Festival, and Silversterklause are only three of the festivals that are described in this book.

Veterans Day
by Jacqueline Cotton (Children's Press, 2002)

This introductory text provides the history and meaning of Veterans Day and offers suggestions for appropriate ways to celebrate the day.

The World Encyclopedia of Christmas
by Gerald, G. Q., and Gerry Bowler
(McClelland & Stuart/Tundra Books, 2000)

This comprehensive look at Christmas around the world includes the religious and secular history, trivia, literature, and art.

Glossary

This is a cumulative glossary of some important terms found in the *Celebrations and Rituals Around the World* series.

A

Abandon To leave or give up a person or object.

Ablution A ceremonial or religious cleansing or washing.

Abolish To destroy or get rid of something.

Abstain To give up doing something; to do without something.

Abundance A quantity that is more than enough, or a great supply.

Adulthood The time of life in which a person is fully grown.

Afterlife Life after death.

Agriculture The science, art, or occupation of cultivating the soil to make crops grow and of raising farm animals.

Altar A table or raised platform on which offerings are placed, usually found in a church, temple, or other place of worship.

Amulet An object, usually a piece of jewelry, inscribed with a magic spell or symbol and worn as a charm to ward off evil spirits or promote good luck.

Ancestor A family member from a preceding generation to whom you are directly related, for example, a grandfather or great-grandfather.

Ancestral Something belonging to a family member from a preceding generation to whom you are directly related, for example a grandfather or great-grandfather.

Annex To take over an area or territory and make it a part of a larger country or state.

Anoint To rub or apply a lotion, often oil, to the skin during a ceremony.

Anthem A song or hymn sung in praise or loyalty to a leader or country.

Ashes What remains of a human body when burned.

Assassinate To kill a leader or political figure.

Astrologer A person who claims to know and interpret the supposed influence of the stars and planets on people or future events.

Astrological ritual A set of actions done in a precise way to predict future events by looking at the position of the stars, which are believed to influence human life.

Asylum A place of safety and protection away from one's homeland.

Atonement The restoration of peace and harmony or favorable relations with God.

Auspicious Bringing good luck.

B

Banquet A feast or formal dinner held on a special occasion and usually for many people.

Bereaved The state of having lost a close family member to death.

Betrothed Promised in marriage.

Bier A stand on which a dead body or coffin is placed before burial or cremation.

Blessing Divine favor or protection. An approval or wish for happiness.

Bourkha A long robe, from the top of the head to the ground, worn by some Muslim women.

Bride price A gift or payment made by a prospective husband or his family to the family of the bride.

Brutal Extremely cruel or severe, causing pain and suffering.

Burial The act or ceremony of placing a dead body in a grave or tomb.

C

Calendar A system of measuring and recording the passage of time.

Campaign A planned operation to achieve a certain goal or end.

Cash crop A crop, such as cotton or tobacco, which is grown primarily for market sale.

Caste One of the social classes into which Hindus are divided.

Catacombs An underground network of passages and chambers that serves as a burial place.

Cemetery A piece of land set aside for the burial of dead bodies.

Ceremony The celebration of an important event with an act or series of acts that follow a set of instructions established by a religion, culture, or country.

Chant To sing in one tone or to repeat a prayer many times. A song or hymn used in religious ritual.

Charm To please, delight, or attract someone. Any object worn or carried by a person, or a word or act, intended to bring luck or avoid evil.

Chastisement Punishment.

Coffin The container in which a dead body is placed to be buried.

Coincide To happen at the same time.

Colonize To establish a settlement in a new country and to impose the newcomers' government or culture on the native people of that country.

Colony A settlement established by people outside their native land and ruled by the mother country.

Commemorate To honor the memory of a special historical or religious event with a celebration or ceremony.

Commemorative An event or object in memory of a special historical or religious occasion.

Communism A political, social, and economic system in which most or all property is owned by the state and is supposed to be shared by all.

Compatible Able to get along with someone.

Condolence The expression of sympathy after a death.

Glossary

Confession The admission of sins or wrongdoings.

Conflict A fight or struggle between two or more opposing nations or groups.

Congregation A gathering or assembly of people usually meeting to worship God or receive religious instruction.

Conquest The act of acquiring something, such as land or territory, by force.

Constellation A group of stars with fixed positions that form an imaginary shape in the sky.

Constitution A document containing the basic laws and principles of a state or nation, and determining the power and rules of a government.

Convent A place where a community of religious people, such as nuns, live.

Convert To change religion or religious beliefs. To become something else.

Convict A person found guilty of a crime and serving a prison sentence as punishment.

Cornhusk The covering of coarse leaves enclosing an ear of corn.

Corpse The dead body of a human being.

Cortege A solemn procession.

Courtship The time when a couple gets to know each other before getting married.

Cremation The act of burning a dead body to ashes.

Crop A large number of plants of any given kind that are grown for human use.

Crucifixion An ancient form of execution that involves nailing or binding a person's hands and feet to a cross. On Good Friday, Christians remember Jesus's crucifixion.

Cultivate To prepare and use land to raise crops by plowing it, planting seeds, and taking care of the growing plants.

Culture A way of life. Every human society has a culture that includes its arts, beliefs, customs, institutions, inventions, language, technology, and values.

D

Deceased Dead. A dead person.

Deity A god or goddess.

Delegate A person acting as a representative for a country or state at a conference or convention.

Descendant A blood relative of a previous generation. A child is a descendant of his or her parents, grandparents, great-grandparents, and so on.

Destiny An imaginary power that determines the future events in someone's life.

Devotee A person who practices his or her religion with strong belief and performs ceremonies and rituals closely following all of that religion's laws and customs.

Devotion Earnestness in religion; religious worship or observance; act of devoting to a sacred use or purpose.

Devout Having strong religious beliefs.

Dialect A local or regional variation of a language.

Dictatorship The term of office or control of a ruler with absolute power and leadership.

Disciple A follower, student, or believer in the teachings of a leader.

Divine Sacred, being related to a god or goddess.

Divorce The legal ending of a marriage.

Dowry Money or property given by a woman or her family to her husband when she marries him.

Drought A shortage of water for a long time.

Dwelling A building used as a home or shelter.

E

Effigy A stuffed figure, which is beaten or burned, that is made to represent a disliked person.

Elder An older person who is respected for his or her experience and wisdom.

Embalm The act of preserving a dead body.

Engagement A promise to marry.

Enlightenment The act of receiving spiritual or intellectual insight or information.

Equality The condition of being equal and treated as equal.

Equinox Either of the two days of the year when the sun is directly above Earth's equator. On these days, the day and night are of nearly equal length everywhere on Earth. The equinoxes occur on March 19, 20, or 21 and on September 22 or 23.

Etiquette Formal rules of behavior in polite society.

Evoke To call forth, bring out.

Exile The state of having been forced to leave one's native country.

Exuberant Full of joy and happiness.

F

Faithfulness A state of being true or trustworthy and keeping a promise.

Famine Shortage of food for a long time.

Farming cycle The period from one planting time to the next in which a series of activities like plowing the land and harvesting is carried out.

Fascism Any system of government in which property is privately owned, but all industry and labor are regulated by a strong national government, while all opposition is rigorously suppressed.

Fast To choose to go without eating for a time, often for religious reasons.

Fate A power beyond human control believed by some to determine the events in a person's life.

Fertility The ability to produce and reproduce living things. Land is fertile when many crops can grow there.

Fertilizer A substance added to soil that adds nutrients and encourages the growth of plants.

Flamboyant Giving a big display or spectacle.

Folklore Legends and beliefs of a group of people.

Glossary

Fortune Happiness or good luck that happens in a person's life.

Fortune-telling Telling or claiming to tell what will happen in the future.

Freedom fighter A person who is involved in armed resistance to an unfair government.

Friar A man who belongs to a religious order.

Fundamentalism A strict religious movement opposed to change based on rigid and traditional principles.

Funeral A religious or other ceremony that usually takes place before a dead body is buried or cremated (burned to ashes).

Furrow A narrow trench made by a plow and in which seeds are planted.

G

Generation People born within the same period of time.

Go-between A person who carries messages and arranges meetings between other people.

Gratitude Thankfulness or the state of being pleased with something received.

Grave A hole dug in the ground where a dead body is buried.

Grief Emotional distress and suffering, especially felt after the death of someone close.

Guardian A person who protects and takes care of another person or object.

Guru In Sikhism, 1 of 10 early leaders of religious faith. In Hinduism, a spiritual teacher.

Gypsy A group of people known for their nomadic lifestyle and whose ancestors originally lived in India. Gypsies live in nearly every part of the world. Some have adopted a settled way of life.

H

Harmony An agreement of feelings, ideas, or actions, or an orderly arrangement.

Harvest The reaping and gathering of grain and other food crops. Also a name for the grain or food that is gathered.

Hearse A vehicle used to transport a coffin.

Henna A dark reddish-brown dye made from the leaves of a tree that grows in the tropical areas of Asia and Africa.

Heritage Tradition, cultural identity, or property passed down from earlier generations.

Homage Respect or honor.

Horoscope A diagram showing the position of the moon, sun, and planets at a specific time, such as when someone was born. A horoscope is said to predict events in someone's life.

Horsemanship The art of riding horses.

Hospitality Friendly and generous treatment of a guest or visitor.

Hygiene The maintenance of health and cleanliness in an individual person and within a group.

I

Icon An image of a god or goddess that is considered sacred and is given special respect.

Ignorance The state of not knowing; lack of knowledge.

Immortal Living forever, never dying.

Immunity The condition of being free of punishment or the harmful effects of sickness or disease.

Incense A material that produces perfumed smoke when burned, usually made from plant products.

Indigenous people The original people living in a country or area before other people settled there, and their descendants.

Infantry Foot soldiers who form part of a larger army.

Initiation The start or beginning of a process, such as admission into a particular society or adult culture.

Insignia A distinguishing mark or symbol.

Intricate Complicated, with many twists and turns.

Isolated Being or feeling alone or separated from others.

Israelites The name by which the ancient Jews were known. Israelites were descendants of Abraham's son Jacob, who was also known as Israel.

J

Jews Descendants of an ancient people called the Hebrews or Israelites who practice Judaism.

L

Labor group A recognized group of workers who are united in their struggle for better working conditions.

Leap year A year that has an extra period of time compared to an ordinary year. In the Gregorian calendar (which normally has 365 days), a leap year occurs every 4 years and has 366 days. The extra day has been added to make up for the extra quarter of a day in the solar calendar.

Legend A story from a time in the past.

Livestock Animals, such as cows and sheep, kept and raised for their produce.

Longevity Long life.

Lunar calendar A calendar that marks the passing of years by following the phases of the moon. Lunar calendars are still used today by the members of some religions and cultures.

Lunar month The period of time from one new moon to the next, which is about 28 days or 4 weeks.

M

Magistrate A government official or judge who is able to apply the law.

Manifestation The act of showing something plainly.

Martyr A person who willingly accepts punishment or death rather than reject his or her religious beliefs.

Masquerade A gathering of people wearing masks and costumes to celebrate a special event or occasion.

Glossary

Matchmaker A person who arranges or tries to arrange marriages for others.

Maturity The stage at which a person becomes responsible for his or her actions and is able to make his or her own decisions.

Meditate To think privately or to focus one's mind on serious or religious thoughts.

Meditation A time of quiet thought and spiritual reflection.

Memorial An object, such as a statue or place, which is a reminder of a dead person or past event.

Merge To be absorbed into or to combine with something.

Messiah Any person claimed or thought to be a savior, liberator, or deliverer.

Midwife A woman trained by schooling or experience who helps women in childbirth.

Migrate To move to a new area or country in search of work or better living conditions.

Minority A group of people with their own identity who are outnumbered by larger groups.

Missionary A person sent by a religious group to preach a faith and to convert others to that faith.

Mock To make fun of a person or thing by imitation or a particular action.

Monarchy A territory or country ruled by a king or queen.

Monastery A place where a community of religious people, such as monks, live.

Monk A man who has separated himself from ordinary ways of life to devote himself to his religion.

Monsoon season The rainy season in India and southern Asia, which is accompanied by high winds.

Mortality The state of being subject to death. The mortality rate is the number of deaths that occur in a given time in a particular community.

Mortar A cup-shaped bowl usually made of stone or marble, containing food ingredients that are to be ground or beaten.

Mortuary A place where a dead body is kept before a funeral. Denoting death or burial.

Mosque A place of worship and prayer for the followers of Islam.

Mourning A period following a person's death during which people express deep sorrow and may perform special rituals in observance of that death.

Mummy A dead body preserved to prevent it from decaying.

Muslim A person who follows the religion of Islam.

Mutiny Rebellion against and refusal to obey authority.

N

Nomad A person who moves from place to place to find food for himself or herself or his or her livestock.

Nun A woman who has separated herself from ordinary ways of life to devote herself to her religion.

O

Officiant A person who performs or leads a ceremony, such as a priest or judge.

Omen A message or event believed to be a sign of what will happen in the future.

Oppression The act of exercising cruel and excessive power and authority over people or a nation.

Orbit The path of Earth or another heavenly body as it circles around the sun or another body.

Orphanage An institution that takes care of and provides shelter for children who have no parents and are homeless.

Oust To remove a person or government forcefully from office and take away their power and authority.

P

Pagan A person who is not, for example, a Christian, Jew, or Muslim, and who may worship many gods or no god. Modern pagans practice some forms of ancient religions.

Pageant A procession or ceremony to celebrate a special event.

Pall bearer A person who walks with or helps to carry a coffin.

Pamper To treat and indulge someone with great care, attention, and love.

Parasol A decorative umbrella often used as protection against sunlight.

Partition The action of dividing a country into separate states or nations.

Patriarch A father or male ruler of a family or community.

Patriotic Full of great love or devotion for one's country.

Penance A religious act that consists of the confession of sins and wrongdoings.

Penitent A person who expresses deep regret or sorrow for wrongs he or she has committed.

Penitential With deep regret or sorrow for sins committed.

Persecute To pursue, punish, or harass a person or group of people. People might be persecuted because of religion, race, or gender.

Persecution The punishment and harassment of a person or a group of people because of their beliefs and principles, such as their religion, or because of their race or gender, or other personal characteristics.

Pestle An instrument used to beat or press a food, such as yams.

Pilgrimage A journey taken to visit a holy place.

Plague A fatal disease that spreads easily and kills many people.

Plot To plan a secret course of action or scheme.

Possess To own. To control or influence.

Precept A rule or law of behavior.

Principle A truth or belief that is a foundation for other truths.

Procession A parade held for a religious ceremony or ritual.

Glossary

Prophet A person who has been inspired by God and communicates God's will or interprets God's message to the people.

Proposal An offer, such as an offer of marriage.

Prosperity The condition of having good luck and success.

Prosperous Successful; thriving; doing well; fortunate.

Protest To make a strong objection against something.

Prow The front part of a ship or boat.

Puberty The stage during which a child physically develops into an adult.

Purification The act of cleansing a person or object, often through ceremony or ritual.

Pyre A pile of wood for burning a dead body during a funeral ceremony.

R

Reception A social gathering to receive and welcome people that may follow a ceremony or formal occasion.

Recite To say something, such as a prayer or verse, to an audience or in a group of people.

Redemption Forgiveness of sins or the freedom from punishment.

Referendum The act of submitting a matter to a direct vote.

Reflection The act of careful and serious thinking.

Reforestation Planting or seeding trees to grow again in an area where they once grew.

Refugee A person who has left his or her community or country to escape danger.

Regent A person who rules or governs a state or country in the absence or inability of the king or queen.

Regime A form of government or administration in which one group of people has total power.

Reincarnation The rebirth of a soul into a new body.

Relic An object that has remained from the past. A sacred object that once belonged to a saint or holy person, kept as a sacred memorial.

Reliquary A small box or container for precious relics and objects.

Repentance Being sorry for doing wrong.

Resemble To look like or be like another person or thing.

Resurrection The act of returning to life after death. On Easter, Christians celebrate Jesus's Resurrection.

Retreat To go back or move away.

Revelation The act of communicating a divine truth.

Reverence A feeling of deep respect or high regard.

Ripen To reach full development and become ready for use.

Rite of passage A ritual or ceremony associated with an event in a person's life that marks a change in status, such as becoming an adult.

Ritual A set of repeated actions done in a precise way, usually with a solemn meaning or significance.

S

Sacrament A ceremony or practice that is an outward sign that a faithful worshiper is receiving God's blessing.

Sacred Holy or precious.

Sacrifice The killing of an animal, which is offered to a god or gods as part of worship.

Saint A holy person who becomes a recognized religious hero by displaying a virtue or virtues valued by his or her religion. A patron saint is a holy person believed to protect the interests of a country, place, group, trade, profession, or activity.

Salutation Greeting.

Sanctuary A sacred place or a place where sacred objects are stored.

Scarce Being restricted in quantity or amount.

Scripture Sacred, religious writing or a passage from the Bible.

Seclusion The condition of being removed and separated from the community and isolated from any social contact with others.

Sect A group of people who share the same beliefs, principles, or opinions.

Secular Worldly affairs, not religious or sacred.

Sermon A public religious speech made by a priest or minister.

Shaman A priest or doctor who uses magic to protect people and to cure the sick.

Sheaf One of the bundles in which grain is bound after harvesting.

Shelter A structure that protects from rain, sun, or danger and is used as a temporary home.

Shrine A small chapel, altar, or sacred place of worship.

Shroud The cloth or garment in which a dead person is wrapped for burial.

Sin An immoral, wrongful act.

Slaughter The killing of animals for food or ceremonial purposes.

Slave A person who is forced to work without pay. A slave is someone who is the property of another person and has no personal rights or freedom.

Solar calendar A calendar that marks the passing of years by measuring the time it takes Earth to revolve completely around the sun, about 365 and one-fourth days. The Julian calendar, established by Julius Caesar in 46 B.C., and the Gregorian calendar, established by Pope Gregory XIII in 1582, are two examples.

Solemn Serious; done with ceremony; connected with religion; sacred.

Solstice One of two moments each year when the sun appears at its northernmost or southernmost position in the sky. In the Northern Hemisphere the summer solstice occurs on June 20, 21, or 22, and the winter solstice occurs on December 21 or 22. In the Southern Hemisphere the solstices are reversed.

Somber Having a serious nature.

Soothsayer A person who claims to tell what will happen in the future.

Soul The spiritual part of a human being.

Sow To plant or scatter seeds.

Spirit A good or bad supernatural being or force.

Glossary

Sponsor A person or organization who takes responsibility for a person or thing or provides financial support for an event.

Stalk To follow or hunt an animal without being seen for the purpose of observing, capturing, or killing it.

Staple Something of primary importance among a community, such as a particular food or crop.

Starvation The condition of having insufficient food to continue living.

Stipulate To express a particular condition or promise within an agreement.

Strike The interruption of work by a group of workers for a period of time to force an employer to meet a demand.

Suitor A man who is courting a particular woman whom he would like to marry.

Sumptuous A word describing a building or object produced at great cost with a magnificent, luxurious appearance.

Supernatural Not of this world; beyond nature.

Superstition A belief or practice that is the result of an unreasonable fear. The belief that magic affects events.

Symbolize To stand for or represent.

Sympathy The sharing of someone's sorrows and sad feelings.

Synagogue A Jewish house of worship and a center of Jewish education and social life.

T

Ten Commandments Ten rules of life given to Moses by God on Mount Sinai, which all Jews and Christians are taught to follow.

Text A body of reading material.

Tomb A structure, often above the ground, where a dead body is housed.

Tombstone A stone or other marker that marks a tomb or grave.

Torah The Hebrew name for the first five books of the Bible.

Tradition The beliefs, opinions, customs, and stories passed from generation to generation by word of mouth or by practice.

Trance A state somewhat like a deep sleep; high emotion.

Treaty A written contract or agreement between two political authorities.

U

Unction The act of anointing a person with oil in a religious practice.

Underworld A world that lies below the world of the living, also called hell.

Unemployment The state of not having a job.

United Nations (UN) An organization of nations that works for world peace and security and the betterment of humanity.

Upheaval A period of great social disorder and disruption that is often violent in nature.

Urge To encourage or press someone to do something in a forceful and persistent manner.

Urn A vase used to hold the ashes of a cremated dead person.

V

Vegetarian A person who eats only plant-based foods and does not eat meat, fish, or some other animal products.

Venerate To honor or to pay deep respect.

Viceroy A person who governs a state or country and acts as the representative of the ruling king or queen.

Vision An unusual appearance of an image or a supernatural form.

Vow A solemn promise made to another person or to God.

W

Wail A long, loud cry because of pain or grief.

Ward off To keep something away.

Widow A woman whose husband is dead and who has not married again. A widower is a man whose wife is dead and who has not married again.

Winter The two hemispheres have winter at different times because Earth is slightly tilted toward the sun. Winter in each hemisphere occurs when that half of the planet is at its greatest tilt away from the sun, so the sun's rays strike it less directly, the days are shorter, and temperatures are cooler.

Wisdom The ability to judge what is right or true. Wisdom often develops with age and life experience.

Withdrawal The removal or retirement of a person or body into a less prominent position.

Wreath A circle of flowers or leaves.

Z

Zodiac An imaginary belt of the heavens divided into 12 constellations or equal parts.

Cumulative Index

This is an alphabetical list of important topics covered in the 10 topic volumes of **World Book, Celebrations and Rituals Around the World** series. Next to each entry is at least one letter code followed by a colon and a number or numbers. For example, in this entry: Ábdul-Bahá, **R:** 31, the letter code **R** tells you what volume to look in for information. The number 31 tells you what page to turn to in that volume. Sometimes a topic appears in more than one place. When it does, additional volume and page numbers are given. Here are the volume names and their codes used in this index:

BG Birth and Growing Up Celebrations
EL End-of-Life Rituals
E Everyday Celebrations and Rituals
H Harvest Celebrations
M Marriage Celebrations

N National Celebrations
NY New Year's Celebrations
R Religious Celebrations
S Spring Celebrations
W Winter Celebrations

Cumulative Index

A

Ábdul-Bahá, **R:**31
Abelam (people), **H:**43
abish (recipe), **E:**41
ablution festivals, **W:**12, 13
Aborigines
  birth and growing up for, **BG:**42, 43
  funeral rites of, **EL:**42, 43
  marriages of, **M:**42
  national celebration of, **N:**42
  religious celebrations of, **R:**42, 43
  spring celebration of, **S:**42, 43
  winter celebrations of, **W:**43
Abraham, **NY:**26, **R:**24, 26-27, 30
Achaemenians, **S:**22
Achetringele (tradition), **NY:**33
activities (projects)
  bridal shower gift, **M:**35
  confetti for weddings, **M:**31
  corn dollies, **H:**27
  dream catcher, **E:**35
  dreidel, paper, **W:**23
  ghost costume, **EL:**33
  guy (doll), **N:**23
  kite, **S:**21
  lantern, **H:**14
  mobile, **BG:**32
  Nativity scene, **R:**33
  paper dreidel, **W:**23

Polynesian lei, **E:**43
  rangoli, **NY:**21
  St. Lucia crown, **W:**28
  stocking for La Befana, **W:**31
  sukkah (decoration), **H:**23
  witch's hat, **EL:**33
  See also recipes
Adam (Biblical figure), **M:**26, **R:**24
address, forms of.
    See etiquette
adolescence. *See* coming of age
Advent, **R:**32
Afghanistan, **M:**22, 23, **N:**8
Africa
  birth and growing up in, **BG:**7, 36-41
  everyday rituals in, **E:**38-41
  funeral rites in, **EL:**38-41
  harvest celebrations in, **H:**7, 38, 40-41
  marriage in, **M:**7, 38-41
  national celebrations in, **N:**7, 38-41
  New Year in, **NY:**7, 38-41
  religious celebrations in, **R:**40-41
  spring celebrations in, **S:**27, 38-41
  winter celebrations in, **W:**40-41
African Americans, **H:**38, **M:**36, **N:**7, 34-35, **W:**34, 35
African National Congress, **N:**41
afterlife beliefs, **EL:**7
  in Africa, **EL:**38-41

in ancient world, **EL:**8-11
  in Asia, **EL:**12, 13, 16, 17, 19-21, 23-29
  in Europe and Americas, **EL:**30, 34-36
  in Pacific Islands, **EL:**42-43
agni (fire), **M:**18
Agni (god), **H:**19, **W:**16, 17
agriculture. *See* farming
Ahura Mazda (god), **EL:**22, **H:**11, **S:**22, **W:**25
Ainu (people), **N:**8
airag (beverage), **W:**14, 15
Akha (people), **BG:**18, 19, **E:**12, **EL:**19, **NY:**18, 19
akhet (season), **W:**8
Akua'ba dolls, **BG:**36
ale, **E:**30
Alexander the Great, **S:**23, **W:**20
Alexandria (Egypt), **W:**20
Algeria, **N:**38
Algonkian peoples, **M:**36
Allah, **BG:**28, 29, **E:**26, **EL:**26, **M:**26, **R:**24-29
  See also Islam
Allahabad (India), **W:**18, 19
All Hallow's Eve, **EL:**33
All Souls' Day, **EL:**31, 36
almond blossoms, **S:**32
almonds, **BG:**24, **M:**31
altars, **EL:**36, **M:**11
Amalthea (myth), **H:**34
Amaterasu-Omikami (goddess), **R:**12
Amazon region, **E:**36, 37, **W:**39
Ambika (goddess), **E:**20

American Indians.
    See Indians, American
American Revolution.
    See Revolutionary War in America
Americas. *See* Canada; Cuba; Indians, American; Latin America; Mexico; United States
Amish, **M:**34
Amon-Re (god), **R:**8
amrit (drink), **W:**19
Amritsar (India), **BG:**22, **E:**21, **M:**20
amulets, **BG:**24, 34, **E:**39, **EL:**42, **M:**43
ancestors
  in birth and growing up celebrations, **BG:**13, 34, 36, 43
  in end-of-life rituals
    in Africa, **EL:**38-40
    in Asia, **EL:**12, 13, 16, 17, 19
    in Australasia and Oceania, **EL:**42, 43
    in North America, **EL:**34
  in everyday rituals, **E:**16, 38, 40, 43
  in harvest celebrations, **H:**14, 15, 22, 43
  in New Year celebrations, **NY:**12, 16, 17, 19
  in religious celebrations, **R:**13, 42
  in spring celebrations, **S:**11, 15
  in wedding ceremonies, **M:**11, 21, 42

See also afterlife beliefs; elders

angels, **EL:**26, 27, 37

Anglican Church, **N:**22

Angola, **BG:**36, 39, **N:**38, 39

Angra Mainyu (spirit), **EL:**22, **S:**22, **W:**25

animal sacrifice
in birth and growing up rituals, **BG:**18, 28, 37, 38
in funeral rites, **EL:**19, 38
in harvest celebrations, **H:**10, 41
in Passover festival, **N:**19
in religious celebrations, **R:**9, 27, 40
in spring celebrations, **S:**32

Anlo (people), **NY:**41

Año Viejo dolls, **NY:**38, 39

Ansari al-Harowi, **EL:**27

Anthesteria (festival), **EL:**10

Antiochus IV, **W:**21

Antyeshti (ceremony), **EL:**20

Anzacs (soldiers), **N:**43

Apache Indians, **BG:**35

apartheid, **N:**40-41

Apollo (god), **E:**9

apples, **NY:**27

April Fool's Day, **S:**32, 33

Aqiqa (ritual), **BG:**28

Arabic, **BG:**29

Arabs, **N:**21

Arahat Mahinda, **R:**17

Ardashir I, **W:**25

Argentina, **E:**36, **NY:**39

Argungu Fishing Festival, **W:**40-41

Arjuna, **R:**18

arkhi. *See* airag

Arlington National Cemetery, **EL:**34, 35

Armenia, **S:**24

Armistice Day, **EL:**32

Artemis (goddess), **BG:**8, 11, **W:**8

Asasa Ya (god), **S:**41

Ashanti (people), **BG:**36, **EL:**38, 41, **S:**40, 41

Ashkenazi Jews, **BG:**24, 25

Ashura (day), **NY:**30

Ash Wednesday, **S:**27

Asia
birth and growing up in, **BG:**12-29
end-of-life rituals in, **EL:**12-29
everyday rituals in, **E:**10-27

harvest celebrations in, **H:**12-25

marriage in, **M:**10-29

national celebrations in, **N:**7, 10-21

New Year celebrations in, **NY:**10-31

religious celebrations in, **R:**10-31

spring celebrations in, **S:**10-25

winter celebrations in, **W:**10-25

Asie Usu (spirit), **E:**38

Asmat (people), **EL:**43

Assumption, Day of, **H:**10

Assyrians, **M:**28, 29

astrology, **M:**8, 10, 17

Athena (goddess), **R:**8

Athens (Greece), **R:**8, **W:**8

Atonement, Day of. *See* Yom Kippur

"Auld Lang Syne" (song), **NY:**32

Australasia. *See* Australia; New Zealand; Pacific Islands

Australia
birth and growing up in, **BG:**42-43
funeral rites in, **EL:**42, 43
marriage in, **M:**42
national celebrations in, **N:**42-43
New Year celebrations in, **NY:**42
religious celebrations in, **R:**42, 43
spring celebrations in, **S:**42-43
winter celebrations in, **W:**43

Australia Day, **N:**42, 43

Austria, **H:**28-29, **NY:**33, 34, **W:**26, 31

avatars, **R:**18, 19

ax, **M:**42

Aymara people, **NY:**7

Ayodhya (India), **N:**17

Aztec, **N:**36, **NY:**8
birth and growing up for, **BG:**9
everyday rituals of, **E:**8
funeral rites of, **EL:**36
harvest celebrations of, **H:**8, 9
marriages of, **M:**8
religious ritual of, **R:**9
spring celebration of, **S:**8

B

Báb, **R:**30-31

babies. *See* birth and growing up celebrations

baby showers, **BG:**32

Baccalauréat (diploma), **BG:**11

Badshahi mosque, **N:**16

Baghmati River, **EL:**20

bagpipes, **NY:**32

Bahá'í faith, **NY:**7, **R:**30-31

Bahá u'lláh, **R:**30-31

Baining (people), **H:**42

Baisakhi (festival), **H:**21

bald eagle (symbol), **N:**32

Bali (island), **BG:**17, **E:**16, **H:**17, **M:**15, **R:**13, **S:**15

Bali (people), **BG:**37

bamboo climbing, **EL:**15

Bangladesh, **N:**16, **NY:**20, **R:**19

Banyankole (people), **EL:**38

baptism, **BG:**7, 10, 30, 31, **M:**34, **W:**30, 41

Barbados, **H:**38

barbecue sauce (recipe), **N:**33

bark cloth, **M:**43

barley, **H:**8, 24, 25, 27, **NY:**24, 25

bar mitzvah, **BG:**26, 27

Barong dance, **S:**15

Basant (festival), **S:**21

baseball, **E:**33

Basil, St., the Great, **NY:**32-35

baskets, **BG:**18, 34, **EL:**34

Bassari (people), **BG:**39-41

Bastille Day, **N:**7, 24-25

Batak (people), **M:**15

bathing, **E:**15, 29, **W:**18-19
See also washing

bat mitzvah, **BG:**26, 27

Baule (people), **E:**38

beach weddings, **M:**42

beadwork, **BG:**41, **E:**37, **M:**40, **S:**37

Bean-Scattering Festival, **S:**13

Bear Dance, **S:**37

Bedik (people), **S:**38

Bedouins, **M:**27

beer, **E:**30, **H:**10, 28, 29

Befana, La (legend), **W:**31

Belarus, **N:**28

Belgium, **N:**38

Bellamy, Francis, **E:**33

bells, **NY:**15, **S:**34, 35
church, **E:**28

Bengal (India), **W:**17

Benin, **BG:**37, 39, **E:**39, **EL:**38, **N:**7

Bentinck, Lord William, **EL:**21

Berbers (people), **M:**38, 39, **S:**40

Berit Milah (ceremony), **BG:**25

Berlin Wall, **N:**28

berserkers (warriors), **BG:**9

Bethlehem (Israel), **R:**32, 33

Bhagavad-Gita (poem), **R:**18

Bhaiya Dooj (day), **NY:**22, 23

bhangra (dance), **W:**17

Bhogali Bihu (festival), **H:**19

Bhutan, **E:**23, **EL:**25, **H:**20-21, **S:**20

Bhutto, Benazir, **N:**16

Bible
in Christianity, **R:**32, 35, **S:**29
in Islam, **R:**24
in Judaism, **EL:**28, **H:**22, 24, 25, **M:**25, **N:**18, **W:**20

binus (shrines), **E:**38

Biri (headdress), **BG:**39

Birla Mandir (temple), **S:**16

birth and growing up celebrations, **BG:**7
in Africa, **BG:**36-41
in ancient world, **BG:**8-9
in Asia, **BG:**10, 12-29
in Australasia and Oceania, **BG:**42-43
in Europe, **BG:**10-11, 30-31
in history, **BG:**10-11
See also coming of age; initiation rites

birthday cakes, **BG:**11

birthday gifts, **BG:**11, 12, 14

birthday parties, **BG:**11

birthdays, **BG:**11-13, **NY:**14, 16

Bismillah (ceremony), **BG:**29

bis poles, **EL:**43

bituun (meal), **W:**15

black, for mourning, **EL:**31

Black Death, **EL:**11

black-eyed peas, **NY:**36

Black History Month, **W:**34, 35

Black Peter, **W:**27

Cumulative Index

blacks (people), **N:**40-41, **R:**39
See also African Americans
blindness, **W:**28
Blood of the Maccabees (flowers), **W:**22
boat races, **H:**20, 42
Bobo (people), **S:**39
Bodhidharma, **E:**14
Bodhi tree, **R:**16
body ornaments, **E:**37, 40
Boers, **N:**40
Bogong Moth Festival, **S:**42
Boi-Bumbá (play), **W:**39
Bolívar, Simón, **N:**36, 37
Bolivia, **N:**37, **NY:**38, **S:**27
bombillas (straws), **E:**36
Bon (religion), **EL:**24, 25
Bonfire Night.
See Guy Fawkes Day
bonfires
harvest, **H:**19, 33
national celebration, **N:**23, 32
New Year, **NY:**8, 9, 32
spring, **S:**18, 22, 23, 25, 34
winter, **W:**17, 25, 33, 34, 39
See also fire
Bon-Odori (dance), **EL:**17
Book of Mormon, **R:**35
boots, **W:**26, 27
Borneo, **H:**16, **N:**12, **S:**7
Borobudur (temple), **R:**13
Bororo (people), **E:**37, **M:**38
Bosnia-Herzegovina, **N:**29
Boston Tea Party, **N:**30
Botticelli, Sandro, **S:**9
bourkhas (garments), **E:**27, **M:**27
bowing (greeting), **E:**15
boys. *See* birth and growing up celebrations; coming of age
bracelets, **M:**15, 28
Brahma (god), **R:**18, **W:**18
Brahman (god), **E:**19, **R:**18
Brazil
everyday rituals in, **E:**36, 37
harvest in, **H:**39
marriage in, **M:**34
national celebration in, **N:**37
New Year in, **NY:**39
religious celebration in, **R:**38
spring celebration in, **S:**27
winter festivals in, **W:**39

bread, **BG:**31, **E:**41, **M:**33, **NY:**27, **S:**31
of the dead, **EL:**37
bridal showers, **M:**31, 35
bride price, **M:**7, 15, 38, 39, 43
brides. *See* weddings
Brides' Fair, **M:**39
bridesmaids, **M:**33, 37
Bridget, St., **S:**8
British East India Company, **N:**14, 15
broom-jumping, **M:**36
Brueghel, Peter, **H:**11
Brunei, **N:**12
Buddha, **BG:**17, **R:**7, 19
festivals honoring, **NY:**24, 25, **R:**13-17
funeral rites and, **EL:**12, 15, 17, 24
in Bahá'í faith, **R:**30
paintings of, **E:**23
Buddhism
birth and growing up in, **BG:**13, 16, 17
end-of-life rituals in, **EL:**12, 15, 16, 18-19, 24-25
everyday rituals in, **E:**13, 14, 16, 20, 22-23
harvest celebrations in, **H:**21
marriage in, **M:**11, 14
national celebrations and, **N:**8, 14
New Year in, **NY:**15, 17, 24-25
religious celebrations in, **R:**10, 13, 14-17
spring celebrations in, **S:**10-14, 20
buffalo, **E:**34
skull of, **BG:**35, **R:**37
buk (drum), **NY:**16
Bulgaria, **NY:**7, 33-35, **S:**43
bull roarers (instruments), **BG:**42
burial, **EL:**7
in Africa, **EL:**40-41
in Asia, **EL:**12, 13, 18-19, 22, 25-29
in Australasia and Oceania, **EL:**42-43
in Europe, **EL:**11, 30-33
in North America, **EL:**34, 35, 37
in prehistoric and ancient times, **EL:**8-11

Burkina Faso, **E:**40, **EL:**40, 41, **S:**38, 39
Burma. *See* Myanmar
Burns, Robert, **NY:**32
Buryats (people), **E:**13
Buthelezi, Mangosuthu, **N:**41
buuz (food), **W:**14
buzkashi (game), **M:**23
Bwa (people), **EL:**40
Byron, Lord, **N:**26

C

Caesar, Julius, **NY:**7, 9
cake
birthday, **BG:**11
harvest festival, **H:**13-15, 25
New Year's Day, **NY:**33
religious festival, **R:**13, 29, 34
wedding, **M:**36
winter festival, **W:**26, 30, 39
calabashes, **M:**38
calaveras (food), **EL:**36, 37
calendar, **NY:**7-9
ancient Roman, **NY:**32
Aztec, **EL:**36, **NY:**8
Celtic, **NY:**9
Egyptian, **H:**8, **W:**8
Greek, **W:**8
Gregorian, **NY:**9, 14, 35
Hindu, **NY:**20, **W:**16
Hopi, **H:**32
Islamic, **NY:**30, **R:**26, 28
Jewish, **H:**24, **NY:**26, 29, **W:**20
Julian, **NY:**7, 9, 35, **S:**30
lunar, **EL:**14, **M:**11, **NY:**9, 10, 14, 30
Mayan, **NY:**38
Mesopotamian, **H:**8
pagan, **H:**11
Ute Indian, **S:**37
call to prayer, **BG:**28
calypso music, **H:**38
Cambodia, **BG:**17, **N:**12, **S:**14
camels, **R:**27, **W:**30
Cameroon, **BG:**36, 37, **E:**38
Cana, wedding at, **M:**32

Canada
everyday rituals in, **E:**32-35
harvest celebrations in, **H:**7, 35
New Year in, **NY:**36, 37
spring celebrations in, **S:**35, 37
winter celebrations in, **W:**7, 36-37
Canberra (Australia), **S:**43
candles
birthday cake, **BG:**11
end-of-life ritual, **EL:**14, 17-19, 28, 33, 36, 37
New Year, **NY:**21, 27-29, 39
religious celebration, **R:**17, 32
Sabbath, **E:**25
spring celebration, **S:**30, 31
winter celebration, **W:**7, 9, 17, 21-23, 28, 29
candy, **EL:**31, 36
canoe prows, **NY:**43
canoe racing, **H:**42
Cape Town (South Africa), **NY:**41
caps, **BG:**18, 19, 26, 32, 33
See also hats
Cardea (goddess), **M:**9
cards, greeting.
See greeting cards
Carmaque (France), **H:**26
carnivals, **NY:**41, **S:**8, 9, 26-27, **W:**36, 39
Caroline Islands, **N:**9
caroling, **R:**34
Carpatho-Rusyns (people), **M:**33
caste system, **M:**19, **R:**23
Castiglione, Baldassare, **E:**9
catacombs, **EL:**10
Catesby, Robert, **N:**22
Catholic Church. *See* Roman Catholic Church
cat shoes, **BG:**12
cattle, **EL:**22, 41, **H:**19, 28, **M:**41
Ceausescu, Nicolae, **N:**29
Celts
birth rituals of, **BG:**9
funeral rites of, **EL:**9
harvest festival of, **H:**10, 11
New Year celebrations of, **NY:**8, 9, 32, 33
New Year for, **N:**23
religious celebration of, **R:**9
spring celebrations of, **S:**8, 34

cemeteries, **EL:**7, 12, 27, 33, 35, 37

Centeotl (goddess), **H:**39

Central America. *See* Latin America

Cerealia (festival), **H:**9

ceremonial houses, **H:**43

Ceres (goddess), **H:**9

chakras (belief system), **E:**20

Chalchiuhtlicue (goddess), **BG:**9

chalices, **E:**28

challah bread, **NY:**27

Cham (dance), **NY:**24

chameleon legend, **BG:**39

Champlain, Samuel de, **H:**35

Chang E (legend), **H:**12

Chang Hsien (god), **BG:**13

chappals (shoes), **E:**18

chariots, **M:**29

charity, **E:**20, 21, **H:**20, 27, 29, 37

Charles IX, of France, **S:**33

Charles, Duke of Orleans, **S:**33

charms, silver, **BG:**12

Charye (ritual), **NY:**16

Chayevo (legend), **S:**37

cheese cake (recipe), **H:**25

cherry blossoms, **S:**12

chests, wooden, **M:**9, 24

Cheung Chau Bun Festival, **R:**11

Cheyenne Indians, **BG:**34

Chichen Itza pyramid, **NY:**38

Chichibu Night Festival, **W:**12, 13

childbirth. *See* birth and growing up celebrations

children

in end-of-life rituals, **EL:**33, 37

in everyday rituals, **E:**15, 33, 40

in harvest celebrations, **H:**12, 14, 19, 24

in religious celebrations, **R:**29, 34, 39

in winter celebrations, **W:**26, 27, 29-31

status of, **BG:**10

See also birth and growing up celebrations

Chile, **N:**37

China, **N:**10

birth and growing up in, **BG:**10, 12-13, 18, 19

end-of-life rituals in, **EL:**7, 8, 12-15, 24

everyday rituals in, **E:**9, 10-11, 14

harvest celebrations in, **H:**12-13, 31

marriage in, **M:**10-11

New Year in, **NY:**7, 10-13, 18, **S:**7, 10

religious celebrations in, **R:**7, 10-11

spring celebrations in, **S:**7, 10-11

winter celebrations in, **W:**7, 10-11

See also Tibet

Ch'ing Ming (festival), **S:**11

Chiyoda (Japan), **S:**13

chocolate, **E:**9, **W:**22

chopsticks, **E:**10, **W:**10

Christ. *See* Jesus Christ

Christianity

birth and growing up in, **BG:**16, 30-31

end-of-life rituals in, **EL:**10, 33, 36, 38

everyday rituals in, **E:**9, 28, 38, 43

harvest celebrations in, **H:**11, 20, 31

marriage in, **M:**9, 14, 28-30, 32, 42

New Year in, **NY:**7, 9, 34, 39

religious celebrations in, **R:**7, 13, 32-35, 37-40, 43

spring celebrations in, **S:**14, 24, 28-32, 34

winter celebrations in, **W:**7, 40, 41

See also Eastern Orthodox Churches; Protestantism; Roman Catholic Church

Christmas, **BG:**11, **R:**7, **W:**7

in Ethiopia, **R:**41

in Europe and Americas, **R:**32-35, 39, **W:**26, 27, 30

in Oceania and Polynesia, **R:**42, 43

Christmas trees, **R:**34, 43

Christophe, Henri, **N:**37

Chusok (festival), **H:**14, 15

Cikunza mask, **BG:**39

cilis (ornaments), **E:**16

Cinteotl (goddess), **H:**9

circumcision, **BG:**24-26, 28, 38, 39, 43

civil rights, **N:**25, 34-35, 40-41

Civil War, American, **N:**34

Claudius II, Emperor, **S:**32

cleaning. *See* purification rituals; washing

cloth-cutting ceremony, **BG:**24

clothing and costumes

birth and growing up celebrations

in Africa, **BG:**39-41

in Americas, **BG:**34, 35

in Asia, **BG:**12, 14-17, 19, 23, 25, 26, 28

in Europe and Americas, **BG:**31-33

in Papua New Guinea, **BG:**43

end-of-life rituals

in Africa, **EL:**39, 41

in ancient world, **EL:**9

in Asia, **EL:**12, 16-19, 28

in Europe, **EL:**31, 33

everyday rituals

in Africa, **E:**39, 40

in Americas, **E:**34, 37

in Asia, **E:**15, 22-27

harvest celebrations

in Africa, **H:**40, 41

in Americas, **H:**33, 38, 39

in Asia, **H:**15, 17, 20, 21

in Europe, **H:**26-28, 30, 31

national celebrations, **N:**9, 24, 29, 36, 42

New Year celebrations, **NY:**7

in Africa, **NY:**41

in Asia, **NY:**10, 11, 17-19, 24, 29

in Europe, **NY:**34, 35

in Latin America, **NY:**38, 39

religious celebrations

American Indian, **R:**38

in Africa, **R:**41

in Asia, **R:**15, 23, 29

spring celebrations

in Americas, **S:**26, 27, 29, 37

in Asia, **S:**13-17, 20, 21, 25

in Europe, 9, 26, 29, 31

weddings

in Africa, **M:**40

in Americas, **M:**35-37

in Asia, **M:**11, 12, 14-17, 20, 22, 27

in Europe, **M:**31

in Pacific Islands, **M:**43

winter celebrations, **W:**7

in Americas, **W:**32, 34, 39

in ancient world, **W:**9

in Asia, **W:**10, 12, 15

in Europe, **W:**29, 30

in Oceania, **W:**42, 43

See also hats; headdresses; jewelry; masks

coconuts, **M:**18

coffee, **E:**26, 27, 30, 32, **NY:**40

coffins. *See* burial

coins, **EL:**31, **M:**31, **NY:**8, 22, **S:**23, **W:**22, 35

cola nuts, **BG:**36

Colombia, **N:**37, **NY:**39

colonies

African, **E:**40, **N:**38-39

American (U.S.), **N:**7, 30, **S:**7, 34-36

Australia, **N:**42, 43

India, **N:**14-15

Latin American, **N:**36-37

New Zealand, **N:**42

Southeast Asian, **N:**12-13

coming of age, **BG:**7

in Africa, **BG:**38-41

in ancient Greece, **BG:**8

in Asia, **BG:**15, 16, 21, 23, 26-29

in Europe and Americas, **BG:**31-35

in Pacific Islands, **BG:**42-43

See also initiation rites

Communion. *See* Holy Communion

Communism, **EL:**13, **N:**28-29, **R:**10

compass, **R:**24

conch shells, **H:**20

Confederacy, **N:**34

confetti (project), **M:**31

confirmation (ceremony), **BG:**31

Cumulative Index

Confucianism
  birth and growing up in, **BG:**16
  end-of-life rituals in, **EL:**12, 18, **R:**10, **S:**11
  everyday rituals in, **E:**11
  marriage in, **M:**14
Confucius, **E:**11, **R:**10
Congo (Kinshasa), **BG:**39, **E:**40, **M:**40, **N:**38
Conservative Judaism, **M:**24
Constitution
  Japanese, **N:**10
  United States, **N:**30
Constitution Day (Thailand), **N:**12
Constitution Memorial Day (Japan), **N:**10
contracts, marriage. *See* marriage contracts
Cook, James, **H:**42
Copenhagen (Denmark), **S:**25
Copts, **NY:**7
corn, **H:**9, 27, 32-34, 36, **S:**36, 37
corn dollies, **H:**27
cornucopia, **H:**34
Corpus Christi (festival), **H:**38, 39, **R:**39
Corpus Domini (festival), **R:**35
Costa Rica, **E:**36, **N:**36, **NY:**38
costermongers (tradesmen), **H:**27
costumes. *See* clothing and costumes
Côte d'Ivoire. *See* Ivory Coast
courting bags, **M:**15
court jesters, **S:**9
covenant bags, **BG:**25
cowrie shells, **BG:**19, 40, 41, **EL:**41
cows. *See* cattle
cradleboards, **BG:**34
cranberries, **H:**37
crane (bird), as symbol, **M:**12
Creation, **M:**40, **R:**36, **W:**20
Creek Indians, **H:**33
cremation, **EL:**7
  in ancient times, **EL:**10, 11
  in Asia, **EL:**12, 13, 16, 19-21, 23, 24, 27, 28
  in Europe, **EL:**30
  in North America, **EL:**34-35

Croatia, **N:**29
Crop Over (festival), **H:**38
cross (symbol), **R:**35, 40, **W:**41
crowns, **EL:**31, **H:**24, 30, **M:**32, 33, **W:**28, 29
crucifixion, of Christ, **S:**24, 28, 29
"Cry of Dolores" (speech), **N:**36
Cuba, **M:**37
cuica (instrument), **S:**27
Cupid, **S:**32
Cybele (goddess), **S:**33
cycling, **E:**33
Czechoslovakia, **N:**28
Czech Republic, **H:**30-31, **M:**33, **N:**28, **W:**27

D

dabka (dance), **M:**27
Dades Valley (Morocco), **S:**40
Dahi-Handi (ceremony), **R:**19
Daikaku Matsuri festival, **R:**12
Dalai Lama, **EL:**24, **N:**8, **NY:**24
damarus (drums), **EL:**24
dancing
  birth and growing up celebration, **BG:**8, 16
  in Africa, **BG:**39-41
  in Americas, **BG:**32-35
  end-of-life ritual, **EL:**17, 39, 40
  everyday ritual, **E:**26, 27, 39, 43
  harvest celebration
    in Africa, **H:**41
    in Americas, **H:**32, 33, 39
    in Asia, **H:**13-15, 17, 21
    in Europe, **H:**26, 28, 30, 31
    in Pacific Islands, **H:**42, 43
  national celebration, **N:**9, 13, 28
  New Year celebration
    in Africa, **NY:**40, 41
    in Asia, **NY:**10, 11, 14, 16, 19, 24
    in Europe, **NY:**8, 34

religious celebration
  in Africa, **R:**40, 41
  in Americas, **R:**37, 38
  in Asia, **R:**7, 10, 21
spring celebration
  in Africa, **S:**39, 40
  in Americas, **S:**37
  in Asia, **S:**10, 14, 15, 19-21
  in Europe, **S:**34, 35
wedding, **M:**7
  in Africa, **M:**38-41
  in Asia, **M:**22, 24-27
  in Europe, **M:**31
winter celebration, **W:**17, 24, 39, 43
Darius I, the Great, **NY:**9
Darwin Festival, **W:**43
Datar (ceremony), **M:**19
dating, **BG:**33, **M:**7, 34
Dawit, **R:**40
Dayak (people), **S:**14
Day of Judgment, **EL:**26, 27
Day of the Dead.
  See Día de Los Muertos
death announcements, **EL:**30
death rituals. *See* funeral rites
Declaration of Independence, **N:**7, 30-32
Declaration of the Rights of Man and of the Citizen, **N:**25
de Klerk, F. W., **N:**41
Delacroix, Eugène, **N:**25, 26
Delaware Indians, **H:**37
della Robbia, Luca, **BG:**10
Delphi, oracle at, **E:**9
Delphic Festival, **R:**8
Demeter (goddess), **H:**8, 9, **S:**9
Denmark, **M:**35, **NY:**33, **S:**25
dervishes, **E:**27, **W:**24
devil, **R:**26
dharma (belief), **E:**22
Día de Los Muertos (festival), **EL:**7, 36-37
Día de los Tres Reyes (festival), **W:**39
diamonds, **M:**9, 34, **N:**38
dice games, **W:**8
Diego, Juan, **R:**38
Dionysus (god), **E:**9, **W:**8
diplomas, **BG:**11
Dipo (ritual), **BG:**40
divorce, **M:**20, 24, 30

Diwali (festival), **NY:**20-23
diyas (lamps), **NY:**20, 21
Djanggawul (god), **R:**42
Djenne Mosque, **NY:**41
Do (god), **S:**39
Dogai (spirit), **S:**42
Dogon (people), **E:**38, **EL:**39, 41
dogs, **EL:**22
dog-sled racing, **W:**37
Dokota (spirits), **S:**38
dolls
  birth and growing up celebration, **BG:**7, 14, 16, 36, 41
  harvest celebration, **H:**27, 32
  New Year celebration, **NY:**38, 39
  religious celebration, **R:**36, 39
  spring celebration, **S:**37
  winter celebration, **W:**27
Dome of the Rock, **N:**21, **R:**25
Dongzhi (festival), **W:**10
doughnuts, **NY:**34, **W:**22
Douglass, Frederick, **W:**35
doves, **S:**32
dowry, **M:**9-11, 15
Dozynki (festival), **H:**30-31
dragon dance, **H:**13, 14, **NY:**11, **S:**15
dream catchers (devices), **E:**35
Dreamtime (myth), **BG:**42, 43
dreidels (toys), **W:**22, 23
driving
  away, after wedding, **M:**37
  learning, **BG:**32, 33
drums, **E:**43, **N:**9, **W:**17
  end-of-life ritual, **EL:**24, 39
  harvest celebration, **H:**38, 41
  New Year celebration, **NY:**11, 16, 34, 40, 41
  spring celebration, **S:**13-15, 41
  wedding ceremony, **M:**22
ducks, **M:**12
Durga (goddess), **R:**20, 21
Dussehra (festival), **R:**20, 21
Dusun (people), **H:**17
Dutch East Indies, **N:**13

E

eagle dance, **M:**22
earrings, **M:**14, 17
Earthmaker (god), **H:**33
Easter, **R:**35, **S:**7, 14, 28, 30-31
Easter eggs, **S:**30, 31
Eastern Europe, **M:**32-33, **N:**28-29
Eastern Orthodox Churches
  bell-ringing in, **E:**28
  birth and growing up in, **BG:**30, 31
  end-of-life rituals in, **EL:**30
  harvest celebrations in, **H:**10
  marriage in, **M:**30, 32
  national celebrations and, **N:**26, 29
  New Year in, **NY:**7, 33-35, 40
  spring celebrations in, **S:**30
  winter celebrations in, **W:**30
East Timor, **N:**12, 13
Ecuador, **N:**37, **NY:**38
education, **E:**33, 40
  birth and growing up celebrations and, **BG:**11, 17, 21, 25, 32, 33
  See also graduation
Edward III, of England, **EL:**11
Edward VI, of England, **BG:**10
eggs, **BG:**13, **M:**12
Egungun Mask Dance, **E:**39
Egypt, **M:**27, **N:**39
Egypt, ancient
  birth and growing up in, **BG:**8, 11
  everyday rituals in, **E:**9
  funeral rites in, **EL:**8, 9
  harvest celebrations in, **H:**8
  Israelite captivity in, **N:**18-19
  marriage in, **M:**8
  New Year celebrations in, **NY:**8
  religious celebrations in, **R:**8, 33
  spring celebrations in, **S:**8
  winter celebrations in, **W:**8

Elder Brother (god), **H:**33
elders, **E:**11, 15, 18
  See also ancestors
elephant, as symbol, **M:**19, **N:**12, **R:**14, 22
Elephant Festival, **S:**17
Eleusinian Mysteries, **R:**8
Elizabeth, the Queen Mother, **EL:**31
Elizabeth I, of England, **NY:**32
El Salvador, **N:**36
Emancipation Proclamation, **N:**34
embalming, **EL:**9, 28
Empire State Building, **W:**32
engagement, 16, **M:**7, 34, 35
England, **E:**9, 30, 31, **H:**34, 35
  harvest celebrations in, **H:**11
  New Year in, **NY:**32
  spring celebrations in, **S:**28, 33-35
  See also United Kingdom
England, Church of, **N:**22
enkangs (enclosures), **M:**41
Epiphany, **W:**7, 30-31, 39
Epona (goddess), **R:**9
equinox
  fall, **H:**11
  spring, **S:**12
Eritrea, **M:**27
Estonia, **N:**28, **S:**7
Ethiopia
  everyday rituals in, **E:**41
  funeral rite in, **EL:**38
  harvest celebration in, **H:**40
  independence of, **N:**39
  marriage in, **M:**27
  New Year in, **NY:**40
  religious celebrations in, **R:**40, 41
  winter celebrations in, **W:**40, 41
etiquette, **E:**7
  in Americas, **E:**32, 36
  in ancient world, **E:**9
  in Asia, **E:**12, 15, 17, 18, 26
  in Europe, **E:**30
  See also hospitality
Etruscans, **EL:**10
Eucharist. See Holy Communion

Europe, **E:**40, **M:**36
  birth and growing up in, **BG:**10-11, 30-33
  end-of-life rituals in, **EL:**30-33
  everyday rituals in, **E:**9, 28-31
  harvest celebrations in, **H:**11, 26-31
  marriage in, **M:**9, 30-33
  national celebrations in, **N:**22-29
  New Year in, **NY:**32-35
  religious celebrations in, **R:**32-35
  spring celebrations in, **S:**7-9, 26-35
  winter celebrations in, **W:**26-33
  See also colonies
Eve (Biblical figure), **M:**26
Evening Star (god), **S:**36
evergreens, **W:**36
everyday rituals, **E:**7
  in Africa, **E:**38-41
  in Americas, **E:**32-37
  in ancient world, **E:**8-9
  in Asia, **E:**10-27
  in Australasia and Pacific, **E:**42-43
  in Europe, **E:**28-31
evil. See good and evil
exile, political, **N:**8
Exodus, **N:**19
Explosion of the Cart, **S:**31

F

Fallas de Valencia, Las (festival), **W:**33
False Faces (society), **S:**36
Fao festival, **H:**41
farming, **NY:**7, **S:**7, 8
  in Africa, **E:**40, **NY:**40, **S:**38-39
  in Americas, **S:**36, 37
  in Asia, **E:**9, 16, **NY:**18, **S:**13-15
  in Pacific Islands, **S:**42, 43
  See also harvest
Fascism, **N:**27
fasting, **H:**9, 33, **NY:**29, 30, **R:**28, **S:**28
Fathers' Day, **W:**33
Father Time, **NY:**37

feasting. See food and feasting
Feast of the Dead, **EL:**34
feet, **E:**15
  washing of, **S:**29
  See also shoes
fertility dolls, **BG:**36
Festa del Papà (festival), **W:**33
Festas Juninas (festivals), **W:**39
Festival of the Dead. See O-Bon Festival
Fetu Afahye Festival, **R:**41
Fiji, **M:**43, **S:**43
Finland, **E:**28, 29, **W:**28
fire
  in end-of-life rituals, **EL:**13, 14, 19, 21, 22
  in wedding ceremonies, **M:**18, 42
  Roman sacred, **E:**8
  walking on, **S:**43
  See also bonfires; candles; cremation; fireworks; lamps; lanterns
fireworks, **H:**12, **W:**13
  national celebration, **N:**23, 25, 33
  New Year, **NY:**7, 34, 39, 40
    in Asia, **NY:**10, 12, 21
    in Australia, **NY:**42
  spring celebration, **S:**10, 17, 22, 31
first footing (custom), **NY:**32, 33
fish icon, **NY:**17
fishing, **W:**40, 41
five K's (clothing), **BG:**23
Five Pillars of Islam, **BG:**29
flagellation, **EL:**11
flags, **W:**19
  Asian, **N:**10, 12, 14-17
  Canadian, **E:**32
  Chilean, **N:**37
  European, **N:**26, 27, 29, **W:**32
  Sikh, **E:**21
  United Nations, **N:**8
  United States, **E:**33, **N:**32, 34
floats, **H:**36, **S:**26, 27, 29, **W:**30, 34, 43
  See also parades and processions
Flora (goddess), **S:**7-9, 34
Floralia (festival), **S:**9, 34
Florence (Italy), **E:**28, **M:**9, **S:**31

Floriade (festival), **S:**43
flowers, **H:**18, **R:**17, 18
  end-of-life ritual, **EL:**13,
    19, 32, 35-37
  in everyday rituals, **E:**17,
    43
  New Year celebration,
    NY:13, 20
  spring celebration, **S:**7, 15,
    23
    in Africa, **S:**40
    in ancient Rome, **S:**8, 9
    in Australia, **S:**43
    in Europe and
      Americas, **S:**32-35
    in Japan, **S:**12, 13
  wedding, **M:**16-18, 20, 34,
    35, 43
  winter celebration, **W:**17,
    22, 32
folklore and legends
  birth and growing up,
    BG:14, 39
  end-of-life, **EL:**15
  harvest celebration
    in Asia, **H:**12, 13, 16-20
    in Europe, **H:**27, 29, 31
  New Year, **NY:**7
    in Asia, **NY:**11, 13, 20
    in Europe, **NY:**32, 35
  religious, **R:**22, 40
  spring
    in ancient Rome, **S:**32
    in Asia, **S:**14, 15, 18, 19,
      25
    in Australia, **S:**43
  wedding, **M:**33, 39
  winter
    in Americas, **W:**37, 39
    in Asia, **W:**18, 22
    in Europe, **W:**26, 27, 31,
      32
  See also gods and
    goddesses
Fon (people), **BG:**37, **EL:**38
food and feasting
  birth and growing up
    celebration
    in Asia, **BG:**12, 13, 16,
      22, 24, 25, 27-29
    in Christian ceremony,
      BG:31
  end-of-life ritual
    in Asia, **EL:**14, 15, 17, 18,
      21
    in Europe, **EL:**31
    in Mexico, **EL:**36, 37
  everyday ritual
    in Africa, **E:**41

in Americas, **E:**32-34, 36
    in ancient world, **E:**9
    in Asia, **E:**10, 12, 14,
      19-21, 23-27
    in Australasia and
      Pacific, **E:**42
    in Europe, **E:**30-31
  harvest celebration
    in Americas, **H:**34, 36-37
    in Asia, **H:**12, 13, 15,
      17-19, 22, 23, 25
    in Europe, **H:**11, 26, 29,
      31
  Jewish national
    celebration, **N:**18, 20, 21
  New Year, **NY:**7
    in Africa, **NY:**40
    in Americas, **NY:**36-38
    in ancient world, **NY:**8, 9
    in Asia, **NY:**12-14, 16,
      23-29
    in Australia, **NY:**42
    in Europe, **NY:**33-35
  religious celebration
    Christmas, **R:**34
    in ancient Rome, **R:**9
    in Asia, **R:**11, 13, 19, 20,
      22, 25, 27-29
    in Australasia, **R:**43
  spring celebration
    in Africa, **S:**38, 39
    in ancient world, **S:**8, 9
    in Asia, **S:**10, 12, 16-19
    in Australia, **S:**42
    in Europe and
      Americas, **S:**9, 27-31
  wedding, **M:**7
    in Americas, **M:**36
    in ancient world, **M:**8, 9
    in Asia, **M:**10, 11, 13, 21,
      24-27
    in Europe, **M:**7, 31
    in Pacific Islands, **M:**43
  winter celebration
    in Americas, **W:**36, 38,
      39
    in Asia, **W:**10, 12, 14-16,
      22, 24, 25
    in Europe, **W:**26, 30, 31,
      33
  See also cake; fasting;
    recipes; wine
football, **H:**36, **NY:**36
foot-binding, **BG:**10
four species (symbol), **H:**22,
    23
Fourth of July.
  See Independence Day
    (American)

fox, as symbol, **H:**15
France, **E:**9, **N:**32
  Bastille Day in, **N:**7, 24-25
  birth and growing up in,
    BG:10, 11
  cemeteries in, **EL:**32, 33
  colonies of, **N:**38, 39
  harvest celebration in,
    H:26
  marriage in, **M:**30, 31, 35,
    37
  spring celebrations in,
    S:27, 33, 34
  winter celebration in,
    W:30
Freedom Day, **N:**41
French Revolution, **M:**30,
    N:24-25
Frey (god), **W:**9
Frobisher, Martin, **H:**35
fufu (food), **E:**41
funeral processions, **EL:**10,
    11, 16, 18, 20, 22, 32
funeral pyres.
  See cremation
funeral rites, **EL:**7
  ancient, **EL:**8-11
  in Africa, **EL:**38-41
  in Asia, **EL:**12-29
  in Australasia and
    Oceania, **EL:**42-43
  in Europe, **EL:**30-33
  in North America,
    EL:34-37
fur trade, **W:**37

G

Ga (people), **EL:**41
Gabon, **BG:**40, **EL:**39, **N:**39
Gabriel (angel), **R:**24, 28, 32
galette des rois (recipe),
    W:30
Galungan (festival), **R:**13
games
  end-of-life ritual, **EL:**15
  New Year celebration,
    NY:15, 16
  winter celebration, **W:**8,
    22, 23, 34, 39
  See also sports
Gamonde (dance), **S:**38
Gandhi, Mohandas K., **N:**7,
    15, 16

Ganesa (god), **BG:**21, **M:**16,
    19, **R:**22
Ganesa Chaturthi (festival),
    R:22
Ganesh. *See* Ganesa
Ganga (goddess), **W:**17, 18
Ganga Sagara (festival),
    W:16, 17
Ganges River, **E:**19, **EL:**21,
    W:17-19
ganggangsuwollae (dance),
    H:15
Ganjitsu (holiday), **NY:**15
Ganna (festival), **R:**41
gardens, Japanese, **E:**14
gargushes (garments),
    M:28
garlands, **M:**16, 20, 43
Gathering of the Chieftains,
    S:7, 41
Gauri (goddess), **R:**20
gay unions, **M:**35
geese, **H:**11, **M:**12, 14
Gelede (society), **H:**40
George III, of England, **N:**30
Georgia (country), **BG:**25
ger (dwellings), **E:**13, **W:**14,
    15
Germanos, Bishop, **N:**26
German Unity, Day of, **N:**28
Germany, **EL:**29, **M:**35, **N:**27
  birthday cake in, **BG:**11
  colonies of, **N:**38
  everyday rituals in, **E:**30
  harvest celebrations in,
    H:28-29
  New Year in, **NY:**33
  reunification of, **N:**28
  St. Nikolaus Day in, **W:**26
geta (shoes), **BG:**15
Gettysburg, Battle of, **N:**34
Ghana
  birth and growing up in,
    BG:36, 40
  end-of-life rituals in,
    EL:38, 41
  harvest celebration in,
    H:41
  independence of, **N:**7
  New Year in, **NY:**40, 41
  religious celebration in,
    R:41
  spring celebrations in, **S:**7,
    41
ghosts, **EL:**14-15, 33
  See also afterlife beliefs

gifts
  birth and growing up,
    BG:10-12, 14, 16, 23, 27
  Christmas, **R:**34
  New Year's, **NY:**12-14, 16,
    23, 35
  wedding, **M:**7
    in Africa, **M:**38
    in Americas, **M:**34-36
    in Asia, **M:**10, 12, 15, 16,
      21, 26
    in Europe, **M:**31
    in Pacific Islands, **M:**43
  winter celebration, **W:**15,
    22, 26, 27, 30, 31, 39
  See also bride price;
    dowry
ginnas (houses), **E:**38
girls. *See* birth and growing
    up celebrations; coming
    of age; women
glass-breaking, **M:**25
go-betweens, **M:**12, 15
Gobind Singh, Guru, **BG:**22,
    23, **H:**21
God, **H:**22, 24, **R:**7
  See also Allah; religious
    rituals and celebrations
godmothers, **BG:**35
gods and goddesses
  in birth and growing up
    celebrations
    African, **BG:**37, 39-41
    American Indian, **BG:**35
    Aztec, **BG:**9
    Celtic, **BG:**9
    Chinese, **BG:**13
    Egyptian, **BG:**8
    Greek, **BG:**8
    Hindu, **BG:**20, 21
    Shinto, **BG:**14
    Thai, **BG:**18, 19
  in end-of-life rituals
    Aztec, **EL:**36
    Hindu, **EL:**20
    Maori, **EL:**42
    Shinto, **EL:**16
    Zoroastrian, **EL:**22
  in everyday rituals, **E:**7
    African, **E:**38, 39
    Asian minority, **E:**13
    Aztec, **E:**8
    Egyptian, **E:**9
    Greek, **E:**9
    Hindu, **E:**18, 19
    Indonesian, **E:**16
    Jain, **E:**20
    Pacific Islander, **E:**43
    Roman, **E:**8

  Thai, **E:**16
  in harvest celebrations, **H:**7
    American Indian, **H:**8-
      10, 32, 33, 39
    Celtic, **H:**10, 11
    Chinese, **H:**13
    Egyptian, **H:**8
    Greek, **H:**9, 34
    Hindu, **H:**18-20
    Indonesian, **H:**17
    Malaysian, **H:**17
    Pacific Islander, **H:**42
    Roman, **H:**9
    Russian, **H:**31
    Shinto, **H:**15
    Zoroastrian, **H:**11
  in New Year celebrations
    African, **NY:**41
    Chinese, **NY:**12, 13
    Egyptian, **NY:**8
    Hindu, **NY:**20-22
    Thai, **NY:**19
  in religious celebrations,
    R:7
    African, **R:**40
    American Indian,
      R:36-38
    Aztec, **R:**9
    Celtic, **R:**9
    Chinese, **R:**10-11
    Egyptian, **R:**8
    Greek, **R:**8
    Hindu, **R:**18-22, 43
    Pacific Islander, **R:**42, 43
    Roman, **R:**9
    Shinto, **R:**12
  in spring celebrations, **S:**7
    African, **S:**38-41
    American Indian, **S:**8, 36
    Asian, **S:**11, 14, 16-18
    Greek, **S:**9
    Pacific Islander, **S:**42, 43
    Roman, **S:**8, 9, 32-34
  in wedding ceremonies
    Chinese, **M:**11
    Greek, **M:**8
    Hindu, **M:**16-19
    Roman, **M:**9
    Shinto, **M:**13
  in winter celebrations
    Egyptian, **W:**8
    Greek, **W:**8, 21
    Hindu, **W:**16-19
    Maori, **W:**42
    Norse, **W:**9
    Roman, **W:**9
    Zoroastrian, **W:**24, 25
  See also religious rituals
    and celebrations

Thai, **E:**16
Gogodala (people), **NY:**43
Golden Temple (India),
    BG:22, **E:**21, **M:**20
gondolas, **M:**12
gongs, **E:**16
good and evil, **EL:**22, **H:**21,
    R:18, **W:**25
  in New Year celebrations,
    NY:12, 15, 20, 21
  in spring celebrations,
    S:18, 20, 22, 39, 42
Good Friday, **S:**24, 28, 29
goose (food), **H:**11
Gorbachev, Mikhail, **N:**28
Gospels, **R:**35
Goths, **W:**9
gourds, **E:**36, 38, **NY:**19, 40
graduation, **BG:**7, 11, 32, 33
Gran Colombia, **N:**37
Grandfather Frost, **NY:**35
Grand Palace (Thailand),
    N:12
Granger, Gordon, **N:**34
granthis (readers), **BG:**22
*Granth Sahib. See Guru
    Granth Sahib*
grapes, **H:**26, **NY:**33, 38
graves. *See* burial
Great Britain. *See* England;
    United Kingdom
Great Spirit, **R:**36, 37
Greece
  Easter in, **S:**30
  everyday rituals in, **E:**30
  Independence Day in,
    N:26
  marriage in, **M:**33
  mourning in, **EL:**31
  New Year in, **NY:**32-34
Greece, ancient
  birth and growing up in,
    BG:8, 11
  everyday rituals in, **E:**9
  funeral rites in, **EL:**10
  harvest celebrations in,
    H:8, 9
  Jews under, **W:**20-22
  marriage in, **M:**8
  New Year celebrations in,
    NY:8, 37
  religious celebrations in,
    R:8
  spring celebrations in, **S:**9,
    32
  winter celebrations in, **W:**8
green, **W:**32
Green Corn Festival, **H:**32,
    33

greeting cards, **E:**15, **R:**29,
    34, **W:**22
  New Year's, **NY:**12, 14, 15,
    21
  spring, **S:**15, 32, 33
greetings
  everyday, *see* etiquette
  New Year's, **NY:**13, 16, 17,
    39, 43
grooms. *See* weddings
Groundhog Day, **W:**34
growing up celebrations.
    See birth and growing
    up celebrations
guacamole, **NY:**38
Guatemala, **E:**37, **N:**9, 36,
    R:38
guedra (dance), **M:**39
Guelaguetza (festival), **H:**38,
    39
guests. *See* hospitality
Guinea, **BG:**39-41
Guisha (god), **E:**13
Gujarat (India), **R:**20, 21
Gunpowder Plot, **N:**22
gunungan wadon (food),
    R:13
gurdwaras (temples),
    BG:22, 23, **E:**21
Guru Granth Sahib (book),
    BG:22, 23, **E:**21, **H:**21,
    M:20, **R:**23
gurus (teachers), **BG:**21, 23,
    R:23
guy (project), **N:**23
Guy Fawkes Day, **N:**22-23
gypsies, **S:**34

H

Hades (god), **S:**9
Haida Indians, **EL:**34
Haile Selassie, **R:**39
hair and hair cutting, **BG:**8,
    13, 16, 21, 23
  See also head-shaving
Haiti, **N:**37
Haji Firuz (troubadours),
    S:22
Hajj (pilgrimage), **R:**26-27
Halloween, **EL:**32, 33
hametz (food), **N:**20
Hamsa (amulet), **BG:**24, 25
Hanami (ceremony), **S:**12
hanboks (jackets), **H:**15

Cumulative Index

Hancock, John, **N:**31
hand decoration. *See* henna
handshaking (greeting),
  E:9, 26, 30, 32, 36
Hanukkah, **W:**7, 20-23
hanukkiyahs (candle-
  holders), **W:**7, 21-23
haoma plant, **EL:**22, 25
"Happy Birthday to You"
  (song), **BG:**11
Harbin (China), **W:**10, 11
Haridwar (India), **W:**19
harmattan wind, **W:**41
harp, **EL:**7
harvest, **H:**7, **NY:**7, 40, **W:**10
  in Africa, **H:**7, 38, 40-41
  in Americas, **H:**10, 32-39
  in ancient world, **H:**8-9
  in Asia, **H:**12-25
  in Australasia and
    Oceania, **H:**42-43
  in Europe, **H:**11, 26-31
  See also farming
Harvest Home (festival),
  H:27
Harvest Moon, Festival of
  the, **H:**12-13
Hasidism, **E:**25
hasta-melap (ritual), **M:**18
Hathor (goddess), **E:**9
hats, **BG:**16, **W:**10, 32
  witch's (project), **EL:**33
  See also caps; headdresses
Hatto, **N:**13
havdalah (ceremony), **E:**25
Hawaiian Islands, **E:**43,
  H:42, **M:**43, **R:**42
hawthorn, **S:**34
headdresses
  in birth and growing up
    celebrations, **BG:**19,
    39-41
  in end-of-life rituals, **EL:**8,
    24, 43
  in everyday rituals, **E:**34,
    40
  in harvest celebrations,
    H:33, 40, 41
  in winter celebrations,
    W:15, 43
  wedding, **M:**10, 27, 28, 38,
    40
  See also caps; crowns;
    hats; veils
head-shaving, **BG:**17, 28, 37,
  39, **E:**23
  See also hair and hair
    cutting

health beliefs
  in Africa, **E:**39
  in Americas, **E:**33, 35, 36
  in Asia, **E:**11, 12, 15, 17, 19,
    27
  in Europe, **E:**29
  in Pacific Islands, **E:**43
heaven. *See* afterlife beliefs
Hebrew language, **BG:**24,
  E:24
Heb-Sed festival, **S:**8
Heh (god), **NY:**8
hei-tiki (Pendant), **N:**42
hell, **EL:**13, 15, 26, 27
henna, **M:**16, 22, 26, 39, 41
Henry VIII, of England, **N:**22
Henry, Patrick, **N:**30
hens, **M:**14
Hera (goddess), **M:**8
herbal medicines, **E:**34, 36
Herod the Great, **BG:**11,
  R:33
Hidalgo y Costilla, Miguel,
  N:36
Higan (festival), **S:**12
"high five" (gesture), **E:**32
Hijra (day), **NY:**30-31
Hilaria (holiday), **S:**33
Hill, Patty and Mildred,
  BG:11
Himba (people), **BG:**37,
  M:40
hime-daruma dolls, **BG:**14
Hinduism
  birth and growing up in,
    BG:16, 17, 20-21
  end-of-life rituals in,
    EL:20-21, 25, **N:**14-17
  everyday rituals in, **E:**16,
    18-20
  harvest celebrations in,
    H:18-21
  marriage in, **M:**7, 15-19
  New Year in, **NY:**20-23
  religious celebrations in,
    R:13, 18-23
  spring celebrations in,
    S:14, 16-19, 33
  winter celebrations in,
    W:16-19
Hispanic Americans, **BG:**32
Hmong (people), **BG:**18,
  EL:19, **NY:**18, 19
Hobson, William, **N:**42
hockey, **E:**33
Hogbetsotso (festival),
  NY:41
Hogmanay (festival), **NY:**32

hokkailos (pouches), **W:**12
Holi (festival), **S:**18-19, 33
Holika (witch), **S:**18
Holland. *See* Netherlands
Holocaust, **EL:**29
Holy Communion, **BG:**31,
  E:28, **R:**35, 39
Holy Saturday, **S:**28
Holy Sepulcher, Church of
  the (Jerusalem), **S:**24
Holy Week, **R:**35, **S:**14, 24,
  28-29
homes
  in Africa, **E:**40
  in Americas, **E:**33
  in Asia, **E:**13, 17, 18, 24
  in Europe, **E:**30
homosexuality, **M:**35
Honduras, **N:**36
hongi (greeting), **NY:**43
Hong Kong, **EL:**15, **H:**13,
  R:11
Hopi Indians, **E:**34, **H:**32, 33,
  M:36, **S:**37
hoplites (soldiers), **W:**20
hora (dance), **M:**25
horoscopes, **E:**29, **NY:**13
horses, **M:**17, 23, 29, **R:**9
horseshoes, and luck, **E:**29
hospitality, **E:**12, 27, 36, 41,
  42
  See also etiquette; homes
Hotei (god), **BG:**14
houses. *See* homes
Hou Yi (legend), **H:**12
Hudoq (dance), **S:**14
Huichol (people), **E:**37
Huitzilopochtli (god), **EL:**36,
  R:9
hula dance, **E:**43
human sacrifice, **E:**8
  in funeral rites, **EL:**8, 21
  in harvest celebrations,
    H:8
  in religious celebrations,
    R:9, 27
  in spring celebrations,
    S:25, 36
Hungary, **E:**29, **NY:**33
Hungry Ghost Festival,
  EL:14-15, **M:**11
huppas (canopies), **M:**25
Huron Indians, **EL:**34
Husayn, **NY:**30, 31
Hussein, Saddam, **S:**25
hyacinth, **S:**23
hygiene. *See* bathing;
  health beliefs; washing

I

Ibo (people), **NY:**40
Ibrahim. *See* Abraham
ice hogs (legend), **W:**37
Iceland, **M:**35
ice sculptures.
    See sculptures, snow
    and ice
ice skating, **W:**11, 37
I Ching (book), **E:**11
`Id al-Adha (festival), **R:**26,
  27
`Id al-Fitr (festival), **R:**29
Ifa ceremony, **E:**39
iftar (food), **R:**28
Imbolc (festival), **S:**8
Imilchil (Morocco), **M:**39
Inari (god), **H:**15
Inca, **EL:**9, **H:**10
incense, **BG:**13, **EL:**22,
  NY:12, **R:**15
Incwala festival, **H:**41
Independence Day
  American, **N:**7, 30-33
  Brazilian, **N:**37
  Greek, **N:**26
  Indian, **N:**17
  Mexican, **N:**36
  Philippine, **N:**13
  Singaporean, **N:**12
India
  birth and growing up in,
    BG:20-23
  everyday rituals in, **E:**18-21
  funeral rites in, **EL:**7, 20-23
  harvest celebrations in,
    H:11, 18-21
  independence of, **N:**7, 14-
    17
  marriage in, **M:**16-21, 26
  New Year in, **NY:**20-24, 31
  religious celebrations in,
    R:7, 16, 18-23, 43
  spring celebrations in,
    S:16-19, 43
  winter celebrations in,
    W:7, 16-19
Indian National Congress,
  N:15
Indian Rebellion, **N:**14
Indians, American
  birth and growing up for,
    BG:7, 34-35
  everyday rituals of, **E:**8,
    34-35
  funeral rites of, **EL:**9, 34,
    36

harvest celebrations of,
H:7, 9, 32-39
marriages of, M:8, 36
national celebrations of,
N:8, 9
New Year celebrations of,
NY:37-39
religious celebrations of,
R:9, 36-38
spring celebrations of, S:7,
36-37
winter celebrations of,
W:7, 34, 39
Indigenous peoples,
national celebrations of,
N:8-9
Indonesia
birth and growing up in,
BG:16
everyday rituals in, E:16,
17
harvest celebrations in,
H:17
independence in, N:12, 13
marriage in, M:14, 15, 42
religious celebrations in,
R:13
spring celebrations in, S:7,
14, 15
Indra (god), H:18
infanticide, BG:10
Ingathering (festival), H:27
initiation rites, BG:7
African, BG:38-41
American Indian, BG:35
Norse, BG:9
Pacific Islander, BG:42, 43
injera (bread), E:41
Inkatha Freedom Party,
N:41
Inning (festival), H:27
International Day of the
World's Indigenous
Peoples, N:8
Inti Raymi (festival), H:10
Inuit (people), R:36
Iran, EL:27, S:25
Bahá'í in, R:31
dress in, E:27
marriage in, M:29
spring celebration in,
S:22-23
winter festival in, W:24, 25
See also Persia, ancient
Iraq, M:28, 29, S:25
Ireland, EL:30, H:11, 27, S:8,
W:32
Iroquois Indians, H:7, 32,
R:36, S:36, W:34

Ishmael, R:27
Isidro, St., H:17
Islam, W:40
birth and growing up in,
BG:16, 28-29
everyday rituals in, E:13,
16, 26-27, 38
funeral rites in, EL:7, 11,
26-27, 38
harvest celebrations in,
H:20
marriage in, M:14, 22-23,
26-28
national movements and,
N:8, 14-17, 26, 29
New Year in, NY:30-31, 41
religious celebrations in,
R:7, 13, 24-29, 31, 40
spring celebrations in,
S:14, 23, 24
Isli (legend), M:39
Israel, M:28, R:30, 31
Easter in, S:24
founding of, N:20, 21
funeral rites in, EL:28, 29
Hanukkah in, W:22
harvest celebrations in,
H:22-25
rites of passage in, BG:26
See also Judaism
Israelites, H:22, 24, N:18-19
Israfil (angel), EL:27
Italy, BG:10, N:27, R:35
end-of-life rituals in,
EL:31, 32
everyday rituals in, E:9, 28,
30
marriage in, M:9, 31
New Year in, NY:33, 34
spring celebrations in,
S:26, 31, 34
winter celebrations in,
W:27, 28, 30, 31, 33
Ivory Coast, BG:41
Izanagi (god), EL:16, M:13
Izanami (goddess), EL:16,
M:13

J

jack-o'-lanterns, EL:33
Jacob (Biblical figure), M:25
jade, EL:8
Jade emperor, R:11, S:10
jaguars, E:37

Jainism, E:20, EL:23, 25
Jaipur (India), NY:23
Jamaica, N:9, R:39
James I, of England, N:22
janggu (drum), NY:16
Janmashtami (festival),
R:18-19
Janus (god), NY:8
Japan, N:8, 11, 13
birth and growing up in,
BG:7, 14-15
Constitution of, N:10
everyday rituals in, E:7,
14-15
funeral rites in, EL:7, 16-17
harvest celebrations in,
H:14-15
marriage in, M:12-13
New Year in, NY:14-15
religious celebrations in,
R:7, 12, 15
spring celebrations in, S:7,
12-13, 43
winter celebrations in,
W:7, 12-13
Jashans (festivals), H:11
Java, R:13, S:7, 15
jazz, EL:35, S:33
Jefferson, Thomas, N:31,
W:35
Jerusalem (Israel), BG:26,
N:21, R:25, 33
Christian celebrations in,
S:24, 28
harvest celebrations in,
H:22-24
Jews' recapture of, W:20-
23
Jesus Christ, EL:30, H:38,
R:7, 30, 39, S:14
Christmas and, R:32-34
Easter and, S:24
Epiphany and, W:7, 30, 38,
39, 41
festivals honoring, R:35
Holy Week and, S:28-30
marriage and, M:9, 32
sacraments and, BG:30,
31, E:28
jewelry, BG:12, 24, 33,
EL:41, NY:18, 19, R:30
marriage and wedding,
M:11, 15-17, 19-21, 28,
38, 40
See also bracelets;
necklaces; rings
Jews. See Israelites; Judaism
jiaozi (food), W:10
Jibril. See Gabriel

jilimis (camps), BG:42
Jingpo (people), E:12
Jingu, Empress, BG:14
Jinnah, Muhammad Ali, N:16
jipeng (dance), S:15
Jishin Balpgi (ritual), NY:16
John VI, of Portugal, N:37
John the Baptist, BG:30,
W:30, 41
Jokwe (people), BG:39
Jol. See Yule
Joseph (Biblical figure), N:18
Joseph, St., R:32-33, W:7, 33,
38
Joya-no-Kane (ritual), NY:15
jubako (food), NY:14
Judah Maccabee, W:20-22
Judaism, R:7, 24
birth and growing up in,
BG:24-27
everyday rituals in, E:24-25
funeral rites in, EL:28-29
harvest celebrations in,
H:22-25
marriage in, M:24-25, 28
national celebrations and,
N:18-21
New Year in, NY:7, 26-29
spring celebrations in,
S:24
winter celebrations in,
W:7, 20-23
Judith (Biblical figure),
BG:24
Jukan (people), EL:38
Juneteenth (holiday), N:7,
34, 35

K

Kaaba (shrine), R:26, 27
Kaamatan (festival), H:17
kachina dolls, H:32, R:36,
S:37
kachina masks, S:37
Kadazan (people), H:17
Kaddish (prayer), EL:29
kadomatsu (decorations),
NY:14
Kalakaua, King, E:43
Kalasha (people), H:21
Kali (goddess), EL:20, R:20
Kalimantan (Indonesia), S:7,
14
Kalki (god), R:19

Cumulative Index

Kama (god), **S:**18, 19
Kamayura (people), **R:**38
kami (spirits), **BG:**14, 15, **M:**13, **R:**12, **S:**13
Kamsa (demon), **R:**18
Kandy (Sri Lanka), **R:**16, 17
Kankouran (spirit), **S:**38, 39
kapparot (ceremony), **NY:**29
karakia (prayer), **BG:**43
Karbala, Battle of, **NY:**31
Karen (people), **BG:**18, **NY:**18, 19
Karo (people), **H:**40
Kasepuhan (people), **S:**15
Kashmir (region), **N:**17
Kashmir Solidarity Day, **N:**17
kashrut (rules), **E:**25
Kassena (people), **H:**41
kat (hat), **BG:**16
kava (drink), **E:**42
Kawa (legend), **S:**25
Kayan (people), **S:**14
Kazakhstan, **N:**28, 29
kemari (game), **NY:**15
Kennedy, John F., **EL:**35
Kenya, **BG:**37, 38, **N:**38, 39
Kenyah (people), **S:**14
Kenyatta, Jomo, **N:**39
Kerala (India), **H:**20, **S:**17
Kern (festival), **H:**27
keters (ornaments), **H:**24
ketubah (contract), **M:**24, 25
Key, Francis Scott, **N:**32
khadags (gifts), **W:**15
Khalsa (brotherhood), **BG:**23
Khanda (symbol), **BG:**22, 23, **E:**21
Khoikhoi (people), **EL:**41
Khomeini, Ayatollah, **R:**31
kibbutzes, **H:**25
Kiddush (ceremony), **BG:**27, **NY:**28
Kikuyu (people), **BG:**38
kilts, **M:**31
kimonos (clothing), **BG:**15, **E:**15, **EL:**16, 17, **M:**12
King, Martin Luther, Jr., **N:**34, 35
King Philip's War, **H:**35
kings, **BG:**10, **EL:**31
kippahs (caps), **BG:**26
kipping (food), **H:**17
Kitchen God, **NY:**13
kites, **NY:**15, **S:**21

kneeling, **E:**9, 15, **M:**34
knishes (recipe), **N:**21
kolams (designs), **H:**18
Kol Nidrei (prayer), **NY:**29
Kong Qiu. *See* Confucius
Konya (Turkey), **W:**24
Koran. *See* Qur'ān
Koré (people), **BG:**39
Korea
   birth and growing up in, **BG:**14, 16
   harvest celebrations in, **H:**14-15
   Japanese occupation of, **N:**10, 11
   marriage in, **M:**14
   New Year in, **NY:**7, 16
kosher food, **E:**24, 25
Krishna (god), **H:**18, **NY:**22, **R:**18, 19, **S:**19
Krobo (people), **BG:**40
Ku (god), **R:**42
Kurds (people), **S:**25
Kurma (god), **R:**18
Kwakiutl Indians, **R:**36
Kwanzaa (festival), **H:**38
Kwoma (people), **H:**43

L

Labor Day (May), **S:**35
labor movement, **S:**35
laddus (sweets), **R:**22
ladybug birthday cake (recipe), **BG:**11
lagan nu custard (recipe), **M:**21
Lahore (Pakistan), **S:**21
Lahu (people), **BG:**18, **E:**12, **NY:**18, 19
Lailat ul-Qadr (holiday), **R:**28
Lakshmi (goddess), **M:**18, **NY:**20-22, **S:**18
lamak (decoration), **R:**13
lamb (food), **W:**14, 15
Lammas (festival), **H:**11
lamps
   funeral rite, **EL:**25
   New Year celebration, **NY:**20-22, 25
   spring celebration, **S:**16, 17
   winter celebration, **W:**11, 20, 21

Lantern Festival.
   See O-Bon Festival
lanterns
   end-of-life ritual, **EL:**15, 17, 33
   harvest celebration, **H:**12, 14, 39
   spring celebration, **S:**10
   winter celebration, **W:**12, 13
Laos, **N:**12, **S:**14
Lao Tzi, **R:**10
lares (spirits), **E:**7
last rites, **EL:**30
Last Supper, **H:**38, **S:**28, 29
Las Vegas (Nevada), **M:**36, 37
Latin America
   everyday rituals in, **E:**36-37
   harvest celebrations in, **H:**9, 38-39
   national celebrations in, **N:**7, 36-37, **NY:**38-39
   religious celebrations in, **R:**38-39
   winter celebrations in, **W:**30, 38-39
   See also Cuba; Hispanic Americans; Mexico
Latvia, **N:**28
Laura Dance and Cultural Festival, **W:**43
laurel (plant), **N:**26, 43
Lavan (hymn), **M:**20
Lebanon, **S:**24
legends. *See* folklore and legends
leis, **E:**43
Lenape Indians, **H:**37
Lent, **S:**9, 26-28, **W:**36
lentil soup, **BG:**29
lesbianism, **M:**35
Liberation Day (Italy), **N:**27
Liberia, **BG:**40, **N:**39
Liberty, Equality, Fraternity! (slogan), **N:**25
Liberty Bell, **N:**32
Lincoln, Abraham, **H:**35, **N:**34, **W:**35
Lion Capital (emblem), **N:**15
Lion Dance, **NY:**10
lip plates, **EL:**38
Lisa (god), **BG:**37
Lisu (people), **BG:**18, **E:**13, **M:**15, **NY:**18, 19
Lithuania, **N:**28
locusts, **N:**19

Lohri (festival), **H:**19, **W:**16, 17
London (England), **E:**31, **N:**22-23
Longinus, **S:**14
Lono (god), **H:**42
Losar (festival), **NY:**24-25
lotus, **M:**10, 11, **R:**18
lotus pose, **E:**19
Louis XIII of France, **BG:**10
Louis XVI of France, **N:**24
love, **S:**8, 9, 18, 19, 32, 33
lovo (feast), **M:**43
Luba (people), **M:**40
Lucban (Philippines), **H:**17
Lucia, St., **W:**7, 28-29
Luciadagen (holiday), **W:**28, 29
luck
   in birth ritual, **BG:**14
   in everyday rituals, **E:**19, 29
   in New Year celebrations, **NY:**10, 11, 13, 33, 39
   in spring celebrations, **S:**17, 23
   marriage and, **M:**10, 11, 13, 25, 36
   See also predicting the future
Ludwig, Crown Prince, **H:**29
Lugh (god), **H:**11
Lughnasad (festival), **H:**11
Lumumba, Patrice, **N:**38
lunar year. *See* calendar
Luo (people), **BG:**36
Lupercalia (festival), **S:**32
Lussekatter (food), **W:**29
Lwalwa (people), **BG:**39
lying in state, **EL:**31

M

Maasai (people), **BG:**37, 38, **M:**41
Mabon (god), **H:**10
Macao, **R:**11
Maccabees, **W:**21, 22
Macedonia, **N:**29
Macy's Thanksgiving Day Parade, **H:**36
Madagascar, **N:**38
Mahabali, King, **H:**20
Mahabharata (book), **R:**18

Maha Khumb Mela (festival), **W:**18, 19

Mahavira (spirit), **EL:**23

mahrs (gifts), **M:**26, 27

mahzor (book), **NY:**28

Makahiki Festival, **H:**42

Makar Sankranti. *See* Pongal

makhlouta (soup), **BG:**29

Malagan (people), **EL:**43

malais (garlands), **E:**17

Malakula Island, **H:**43

Malan, Daniel F., **N:**40

Malanka (festival), **NY:**35

Malaysia, **H:**16, 17, **M:**14, 15, **N:**12, **R:**14, **S:**14

Mali, **E:**38, 40, **EL:**39, **NY:**41

mamoul (cakes), **R:**29

mandala (symbol), **E:**22

mandaps (canopies), **M:**18, 19

Mandela, Nelson, **N:**40, 41

mandirs (temples), **S:**16, 17

mangoes, **M:**21, **R:**20

manna, **H:**22

Manuelitos (figures), **R:**39

Maori (people)

birth and growing up for, **BG:**43

everyday rituals of, **E:**42, 43

funeral rites of, **EL:**42

national celebration of, **N:**42

New Year for, **NY:**42, 43

winter celebration of, **W:**42

Mao Zedong, **EL:**13

Maple Festival, **S:**36

maple syrup, **E:**32

marae (house), **E:**42, **EL:**42

Mardi Gras, **S:**27

Marie Antoinette, **N:**24

Maronite Church, **S:**24

Maroons (people), **N:**9

marriage, **H:**19, **M:**7

arranged, **M:**7-10, 12, 19, 27, 40

civil, **M:**30, 36, 37

See also weddings

marriage contracts

in Africa, **M:**38

in ancient world, **M:**8

in Asia, **M:**15, 22-28

in Europe, **M:**30

in Pacific Islands, **M:**43

"Marseillaise" (song), **N:**25

Martin, St., of Tours, **H:**11

Martin Luther King, Jr., Day, **N:**34, 35

Martinmas (feast day), **H:**11

martorana (candy), **EL:**31

martyrs, **NY:**31

Mary, Virgin, **EL:**30, **H:**39, **R:**41, **S:**34, **W:**33, 38

at Cana marriage, **M:**32

festivals honoring, **H:**10, **R:**38

Nativity and, **R:**32-33

Marys, Two, **S:**34

masi (cloth), **M:**43

Maska (festival), **R:**40

masks

birth and growing up celebration, **BG:**39, 40

end-of-life ritual, **EL:**9, 39-41, 43

everyday ritual, **E:**39, 43

harvest celebration

African, **H:**40, 41

American Indian, **H:**7, 10, 32, 33

Asian, **H:**15, 16, 21

Latin American, **H:**38

Pacific Islander, **H:**42, 43

New Year celebration, **NY:**24, 33, 39

religious celebration, **R:**36, 41, 42

spring celebration

African, **S:**38, 39

American Indian, **S:**36

Asian, **S:**13-15, 20

carnival, **S:**26, 27

Pacific Islander, **S:**42

winter celebration, **W:**31, 38, 42

masquerades, **EL:**39, 40

Mass (ritual), **BG:**31, 32, **E:**28, **R:**35

Easter, **S:**24, 30, 31

marriage, **M:**30

Massachusetts, **H:**34, 35

Massasoit, Chief, **H:**34, 35

Matariki (festival), **NY:**43

matchmakers, **M:**7, 11, 14

maté (drink), **E:**36

Matsés (people), **E:**36, 37

matsuri (ceremonies), **R:**12

Matsya (god), **R:**19

Matthew, St., **R:**40

matzo (food), **N:**18

Maui (god), **R:**42

Maundy Thursday, **S:**24, 28, 29, 31

Mauni Amavasya (festival), **W:**18

Mawlid (festival), **R:**25

Mawu (goddess), **BG:**37

May (month), **S:**34-35

Maya, **E:**8, 37, **N:**9, **NY:**38

May Day, **S:**9, 34-35

Mayflower (ship), **H:**34, 35

Maypole dance, **S:**35

meat, eating of, **E:**19, 25, 26

Mecca (city), **BG:**29, **E:**26, **EL:**11, 26, 27, **NY:**30, **R:**24-27

Medina (city), **EL:**11, 26, **NY:**30, **R:**25

meditation, **E:**11, 14, 20, 22

mehndi. *See* henna

Melanesia, **E:**42, 43, **S:**42

Memorial Day, **EL:**35

menorahs. *See* hanukkiyahs

menstruation, **BG:**34, 40

Meotoiwa (rocks), **M:**13

Merdeka Day, **N:**12

Mesopotamia, **EL:**7, **H:**8, **M:**29, **NY:**8, **R:**24

Mevlâna, **W:**24

Mevlevi Sufi Brotherhood, **W:**24

Mexico

end-of-life rituals in, **EL:**7, 36-37

everyday rituals in, **E:**9, 36, 37

harvest celebrations in, **H:**8, 9, 38, 39

marriage in, **M:**8

national celebration in, **N:**36

New Year in, **NY:**8, 38, 39

religious celebrations in, **R:**38

winter celebrations in, **W:**38, 39

mezuzahs (scrolls), **E:**24

Michael, St., **H:**11, **W:**41

Michaelmas (feast day), **H:**11

Micronesia, **E:**42, 43, **N:**9

Mictlantecuhtli (god), **EL:**36

Middle Ages

baptism in, **BG:**10

end-of-life rituals in, **EL:**10, 11, 30, 33

everyday rituals in, **E:**9, 28, 30

harvest celebrations in, **H:**11

marriage in, **M:**9

St. Joseph's Day in, **W:**33

spring celebrations in, **S:**8, 9, 34

Middle East

birth and growing up in, **BG:**24-29

end-of-life rituals in, **EL:**26-29

everyday rituals in, **E:**27-29

harvest celebrations in, **H:**22-25

marriage in, **M:**24-29

national celebrations in, **N:**18-21

New Year in, **NY:**26-31

religious celebrations in, **R:**24-31

spring celebrations in, **S:**22-25

winter celebrations, **W:**20-25

Midwinter Ceremony, **W:**34

midwives, **R:**38

Mien (people), **BG:**18, 19, **NY:**18, 19

Mienu (festivities), **M:**22

mikoshi (shrines), **BG:**15, **H:**15

Mikulas Day, **W:**27

Milamala yam harvest festival, **H:**43

milk, **H:**25

millet, **E:**41, **S:**39

Min (god), **H:**8

Mina (city), **R:**26

Minangkabau (people), **E:**17

Ming, Emperor, **S:**10

minutemen, **N:**31

Minymor Festival, **S:**38

misri (ceremony), **M:**16

Mitzvot (rules), **M:**24

Mixtecs (people), **E:**9

mizusashi (container), **E:**14

mobile (project), **BG:**32

mochi (food), **NY:**14

mohels (religious officials), **BG:**25

Moldova, **N:**28

money hats, **M:**27

Mongolia, **W:**7, 14-15

Mongols, **E:**13, **H:**13

monks, **BG:**17, **E:**20, 22-23

Mool Mantra (prayer), **BG:**22, 23

moon, **H:**12-14, **NY:**31, 43, **R:**14, 22

See also calendar

moon cakes, **H:**13, 14

Moon Spirit, **R:**36

Moors, **S:**35

Cumulative Index

Moravia, **BG:**24, **H:**30
morin huur (instrument), **W:**15
Moriones Festival, **S:**14
Mormons, **R:**35
Morning Star (god), **S:**36
Morocco, **M:**38, 39, **S:**40
Morris dancing, **S:**34, 35
Moses, **H:**22, 24, **N:**18, 19, **R:**30, **W:**41
mosques, **E:**7, **M:**22, **NY:**31, 41, **R:**25, 28
moths, **S:**42
Mount Arafat, **R:**26
Mount Hagen, **W:**42
Mount Kailas, **EL:**25
Mount of Olives, **EL:**29
Mount Rushmore, **W:**35
Mount Sinai, **H:**24
mourning, **EL:**7
  in Africa, **EL:**41
  in Asia, **EL:**13, 18, 23, 25, 27, 28
  in Europe, **EL:**31
  in North America, **EL:**35
Muhammad, **EL:**11, 26, **NY:**30, 31, 41, **R:**13, 30
  festivals honoring, **R:**24-29
Muharram (day), **NY:**30, 31
Mu Lian, **EL:**15
Mummers' Parade, **NY:**36
mummies, **EL:**8, 9
Munich (Germany), **H:**28, 29
murtis (images), **E:**18, 19
Murukan (god), **R:**43
music
  Christmas, **R:**34
  end-of-life ritual, **EL:**35, 39, 40, 42
  everyday ritual, **E:**17, 43
  harvest celebration, **H:**30, 38, 41-43
  national celebration, **N:**25, 32, 33, 42
  New Year celebration, **NY:**19, 32, 34, 41
  spring celebration
    in Africa, **S:**40, 41
    in Asia, **S:**13-17, 19, 20, 22
    in Europe and Americas, **S:**27, 29, 33
  wedding
    in Asia, **M:**10, 17, 20, 22, 23, 26, 29
    in Europe, **M:**30, 31
  winter celebration, **W:**15, 24, 35, 42, 43
  See also dancing; drums; parades and processions

Muslim League, **N:**16
Muslims. See Islam
Mussolini, Benito, **N:**27
Mwaka Mpya (festival), **NY:**41
Myanmar, **BG:**17, 18, **E:**22, **N:**12, **S:**14
myth. See folklore and legends; gods and goddesses

N

Naked Men festivals, **W:**13
Namakarana samskara (ceremony), **BG:**20
namaste (gesture), **E:**18
Namibia, **BG:**37, **EL:**41, **M:**40
naming, **BG:**7
  in Africa, **BG:**36, 37
  in ancient Rome, **BG:**9
  in Asia, **BG:**12, 18-20, 22, 24-26
  in Europe and Americas, **BG:**30, 34
Nanai (people), **H:**31
Nanak, Guru, **BG:**23, **M:**20, **R:**23
Naomi (Biblical figure), **H:**25
Napoleon I, **BG:**11
Narasimha (god), **R:**19
Narayan (god), **W:**18
national celebrations, **N:**7
  in Africa, **N:**33-41
  in Americas, **N:**30-37
  in Asia, **N:**7, 10-21
  in Australasia and Oceania, **N:**42-43
  in Europe, **N:**22-29
  of indigenous peoples, **N:**8-9
Native Americans. See Indians, American
Nativity, **R:**32, 33, 39
Navagraha puja (ceremony), **M:**17
Navajo Indians, **E:**35
Navaratri (festival), **R:**20, 21
Nawruz (festival), **NY:**9, **R:**31, **S:**22-23
Nazik (India), **W:**19
Nazis, **EL:**29

Ndebele (people), **BG:**41, **E:**40
Neanderthals, **EL:**8
necklaces, **M:**7, 19, 40, 41
neck rings, **BG:**18
Nehru, Jawaharlal, **N:**14, 15, 17
Nepal, **EL:**20, **NY:**24
Netherlands, **H:**34, **N:**13, **S:**43
  everyday rituals in, **E:**30
  marriage in, **M:**31, 35
  New Year in, **NY:**33, 34
  Sinterklaas in, **W:**27
Neto, Antonio Agostinho, **N:**38
New Caledonia, **S:**42
New Guinea, **R:**42
New Ireland, **EL:**43
New Orleans (Louisiana), **EL:**35, **S:**27
  Jazz & Heritage Festival in, **S:**33
Newroz (festival), **S:**25
New Year, **NY:**7, **S:**7
  in Africa, **H:**40, **NY:**7, 40-41
  in Americas, **NY:**36-39
  in ancient world, **NY:**8-9
  in Asia, **NY:**7, 10-31
    Assyrian, **M:**29
    Bahá'í, **R:**31
    Chinese, **NY:**10-13, 18, **S:**7, 10
    Mongolian, **W:**14
    Persian, **S:**23
    Vietnamese, **S:**15
  in Australasia and Oceania, **NY:**42-43
  in Europe, **NY:**34-35
New Year's Eve ball, **NY:**37
New York City, **H:**36, **NY:**37, **W:**32
New Zealand
  birth and growing up in, **BG:**43
  everyday rituals in, **E:**42
  marriage in, **M:**42
  national celebrations in, **N:**42-43
  New Year in, **NY:**42, 43
  religious celebrations in, **R:**42, 43
  winter celebrations in, **W:**42
Ngani (dance), **BG:**39
Ngaseuk ritual, **S:**15
Ngoron (dance), **BG:**41
Nian Monster, **NY:**11
Niathoma (spirit), **S:**38

Nicaragua, **N:**36
Nicholas, St., **W:**26-27
Niger, **M:**38
Nigeria, **E:**39, **EL:**38, **H:**7, **N:**38, **NY:**40, **W:**40
Nikah (ceremony), **M:**23, 26
Nikolaus, St., **W:**26
ninots (models), **W:**33
nirvana, **R:**15-17
Nkrumah, Kwame, **N:**7
Noche de los Rabanos (festival), **W:**38
nomads, **M:**27, 38, 39
noodles, **BG:**13
Norsemen. See Vikings
Northern Hemisphere, **W:**7
Norway, **M:**35, **W:**28
Nukuma (people), **H:**43
nuns, **E:**9, 20, 22-23
Nut (god), **W:**8
Nu Wa (goddess), **M:**11
Nyame (god), **S:**40, 41
Nyigbla (god), **NY:**41

O

Oaxaca (Mexico), **H:**39, **W:**38
O-Bon Festival, **EL:**7, 16-17
Obzinky (festival), **H:**31
Ocalan, Abdullah, **S:**25
Oceania. See Pacific Islands
Odin (god), **W:**9
offerings. See sacrifice
O'Higgins, Bernardo, **N:**37
Oktoberfest (festival), **H:**28, 29
Olympic Festival, **R:**8
Om (chant), **BG:**20
omens. See predicting the future
Omer (interval), **H:**24
omikuji (fortunes), **NY:**15
Onam (festival), **H:**20
ondjongo (dance), **M:**40
Oni (demons), **S:**13
oracles, **E:**9
orange blossoms, **M:**30
oranges, **NY:**12, **W:**26
ordination, Buddhist, **BG:**17
orphans, **BG:**10
Orthodox Judaism, **BG:**24, **E:**24, 25, **M:**24
Oruro (Bolivia), **S:**27
Orvieto, Cathedral of, **R:**35

osechi-ryori (food), **NY:**14
Oshogatsu (festival), **NY:**14
Ottawa (Ontario), **W:**37
Ottoman Empire, **BG:**28,
  N:26
Our Lady of Guadalupe
  (holiday), **R:**38
Our Lady of the Harvest,
  Feast of, **H:**10
oxen, **H:**16, 28

P

Pacific Islands
  birth and growing up in,
    BG:42-43
  end-of-life rituals in,
    EL:42-43
  everyday rituals in, **E:**42-
    43
  harvest celebrations in,
    H:42-43
  marriage in, **M:**42-43
  national celebrations in,
    N:7, 42-43
  New Year in, **NY:**42-43
  religious celebrations in,
    R:42-43
  spring celebrations in,
    S:42-43
  winter celebrations in,
    W:42-43
Padmasambhava, **S:**20
paganism, **H:**11, **NY:**7, 32,
  34, **S:**32
  See also gods and
    goddesses
pahiyas (food), **H:**17
painting
  bark, **M:**42
  of skin, **EL:**20, 42, 43,
    M:41
  sand, **E:**22, 35
  silk, **E:**23
  yam, **E:**37
  See also henna
Pakistan, **BG:**29, **H:**20-21,
  M:22, **N:**16-17, **S:**21
pakoras (recipe), **S:**19
Pak Tai (god), **R:**11
Palestine, **N:**21
Palestine Liberation
  Organization, **N:**21
Palestinians, **M:**27, **N:**21
Pali Canon, **E:**22

Palm Sunday, **S:**24, 28
Pancake Day, **S:**28
pancakes (recipe), **S:**29
Panthenaic Festival, **R:**8
Papago Indians, **H:**33
Papua, **EL:**43, **M:**42
Papua New Guinea
  birth and growing up in,
    BG:7, 43
  death rituals in, **EL:**7, 43
  harvest celebration in,
    H:42, 43
  marriage in, **M:**43
  New Year in, **NY:**43
  winter festival in, **W:**42
parades and processions
  birth and growing up cel-
    ebration, **BG:**15, 34, 41
  harvest
    in Americas, **H:**36, 38, 39
    in Asia, **H:**12, 14, 15, 17,
      21
    in Europe, **H:**28-30
  national celebration
    in Africa, **N:**39
    in Americas, **N:**32, 33, 35
    in Asia, **N:**11, 13, 17
    in France, **N:**25
  New Year's, **NY:**7
    in Americas, **NY:**36, 38
    in ancient Persia, **NY:**9
    in Asia, **NY:**12, 31
    in Europe, **NY:**32, 33, 35
  religious celebration, **R:**7
    in Africa, **R:**41
    in ancient Greece, **R:**8
    in Asia, **R:**11, 13, 15, 17,
      18, 21, 25
    in Australia, **R:**43
    in Latin America, **R:**39
  spring
    in Africa, **S:**41
    in Europe and
      Americas, **S:**26-31, 34,
      35
    in Japan, **S:**13
  winter celebration
    in Africa, **W:**41
    in Americas, **W:**34, 36,
      38
    in Asia, **W:**19
    in Australia, **W:**43
    in Europe, **W:**27, 29-31
  See also funeral
    processions; weddings
Paraguay, **E:**36
Paranirvana (festival), **R:**16,
  17

Parashurama (god), **R:**19
Parintins Jungle Carnival,
  W:39
Paris (France), **EL:**33
Parks, Rosa, **W:**35
Parliament (United
  Kingdom), **N:**22, 30
Paro Tshechu Festival, **S:**20
Parsis (people), **EL:**7, 22,
  H:11, **M:**20-21
Parvati (goddess), **R:**20, 22,
  S:18
Passover, **H:**24, **N:**18-20
Patrick, St., **W:**7, 32
Pavlova (recipe), **N:**43
Pawnee Indians, **S:**36
Pearl Harbor attack, **N:**10
Pedro I, of Brazil, **N:**37
Pedro II, of Brazil, **N:**37
penance (ritual), **BG:**31
pendant, **EL:**41
Pende (people), **BG:**7
Perchtenlaufen (festival),
  W:31
peret (season), **W:**8
Persephone (goddess), **S:**9
Persepolis (city), **S:**22
Persia, ancient, **H:**11, **NY:**9,
  R:30, **S:**22-23, **W:**24, 25
Peru, **E:**36, **H:**10, **N:**37, **R:**39
pharaohs, of Egypt, **E:**9,
  N:18, 19
Philadelphia
  (Pennsylvania), **NY:**36
Philip, King, **H:**35
Philippines
  birth and growing up in,
    BG:16
  greeting in, **E:**17
  harvest celebrations in,
    H:16, 17
  independence of, **N:**12,
    13
  marriage in, **M:**14
  spring celebrations in,
    S:14
Phillip, Arthur, **N:**43
picnics, **S:**12, 23
pie, **H:**37
pigs, **H:**9
pilgrimage, **EL:**11, 21, 25,
  26, **R:**26-27, 30
Pilgrims, **H:**7, 34-36
Pima Indians, **H:**33
piñatas, **R:**39
pindas (food), **EL:**21
pineapple dance, **H:**39
Pipe Carrier (official), **M:**36

plague, **EL:**10, 11
plagues, in Egypt, **N:**19
Plains Indians, **E:**34, **EL:**34,
  S:37
Planting Festival, **S:**36
Pledge of Allegiance, **E:**33
Pleiades (star cluster),
  NY:43
plowing ceremony, **H:**16
Plymouth Colony, **H:**34, 35
Poland, **H:**30, **M:**33, **N:**29
Polar Bear Clubs, **NY:**37,
  W:11
Polynesia, **E:**42, 43, **R:**42-43,
  W:42
Pombibele (statue), **EL:**40
pomegranates, **NY:**26
Pomo Indians, **BG:**34
Pompeii, **M:**9
Pongal (festival), **H:**18-19
pongal pudding, **H:**18, 19
Pooram (festival), **S:**16, 17
poppies, **EL:**32
Portugal, **N:**36-38, **S:**33
Posadas, Las (festival),
  W:38
Poseidon (god), **W:**8
Poson Day, **R:**17
Posviceni (festival), **H:**31
Powamu ceremony, **S:**37
powwows (meetings),
  BG:34, **S:**37
Prahlad (legend), **S:**18
prayer. *See* funeral rites;
  religious rituals and
  celebrations; *and specific
  religions*
prayer beads, **R:**23
prayer flags, **EL:**25, **NY:**25
Prayerstick Festival, **H:**33
prayer wheels, **E:**22
predicting the future, **E:**9,
  11, 29, 39
  See also luck
pregnancy, **BG:**24, 42
prehistoric people, **EL:**8
Presidents' Day, **W:**34, 35
Presley, Elvis, **EL:**35
processions. *See* funeral
  processions; parades
  and processions;
  weddings
projects. *See* activities
pronubas (matrons), **M:**7
prophets and prophet-
  esses, **E:**9, **R:**7, 24
proposal, marriage, **M:**34
Protestantism, **BG:**30, 31,
  H:34, **M:**30

Cumulative Index

Pu (festival), **H:**21
pubs, **E:**30
pudding, **H:**18, 19
Pueblo Indians, **EL:**34, **N:**8, **R:**36, 37
puja (prayer), **E:**18, 19, 22, **H:**18, 19, **M:**16, 17, **NY:**22
Pukimani (rituals), **EL:**43
pumpkin pie, **H:**36, 37
Punjab (India), **N:**17, **W:**16, 17
puppet plays, **E:**17
Pure Brightness, Festival of, **S:**11
purification rituals
  birth and growing up, **BG:**7
    in Africa, **BG:**38, 39
    in ancient world, **BG:**8, 9
    in Asia, **BG:**13, 14, 20
    in Australia, **BG:**42
    in Europe and Americas, **BG:**10, 30, 34
  end-of-life, **EL:**19-22, 26, 37
  everyday, **E:**19, 26, 35
  harvest, **H:**18, 19, 23, 33, 41
  New Year, **NY:**10, 20, 28, 29
  spring, **S:**11, 23, 38-39
  wedding, **M:**18, 21
  winter, **W:**13
  See also bathing; washing
Puritanism, **H:**34
pyramids, Egyptian, **EL:**9

Q

Qatar, **M:**26
Quebec Winter Carnival, **W:**36
queens, **EL:**31
Qufu (China), **R:**10
Quiché Indians, **N:**9
Quinceañera (ceremony), **BG:**32
Qur'ān, **EL:**26, **NY:**31
  in birth and growing up, **BG:**28, 29
  in everyday rituals, **E:**26, 27
  marriage and, **M:**22, 23, 26

R

rababs (instruments), **M:**23
rabbis, **M:**24, 25, 28, **N:**20
Rachel (Biblical figure), **M:**25
Radha (legend), **S:**19
radishes, **W:**38
Raffles, Sir Thomas Stamford, **N:**12
rain, **H:**32, 33, **NY:**37
Rainbow Serpent (legend), **S:**43
Rainmaking Ceremony, **S:**43
Raj (government), **N:**14, 15
Rama (god), **NY:**20, 21, **R:**19, 21
Ramadan (month), **M:**22, **R:**28-29
Ramayana (text), **NY:**20
Ram Das, Guru, **M:**20
ramen (food), **W:**12
Ramses II, **EL:**8, **N:**18
Rangda (witch), **S:**15
rangoli (decorations), **NY:**21
Rashaida bedouins, **M:**27
Rastafarianism, **R:**39
Ravana (demon), **R:**21
recipes
  abish, **E:**41
  barbecue sauce, **N:**33
  bread of the dead, **EL:**37
  buuz (dumplings), **W:**14
  challah bread, **NY:**27
  cheese cake, **H:**25
  Christmas cake, **R:**34
  confetti, **M:**31
  Easter eggs, **S:**31
  galette des rois (cake), **W:**30
  guacamole, **NY:**38
  knishes, **N:**21
  ladybug birthday cake, **BG:**11
  lagan nu custard, **M:**21
  lentil soup (makhlouta), **BG:**29
  mango sorbet, **R:**20
  noodles, long-life, **BG:**13
  pakoras, **S:**19
  pancakes, **S:**29
  Pavlova, **N:**43
  pumpkin pie, **H:**37
  St. Basil's Cake, **NY:**33
  scones, **E:**31
  vegetables, **EL:**15

redcoats, **N:**31
Reform Judaism, **BG:**24, **M:**24
reincarnation, **EL:**23
religious rituals and celebrations, **E:**7, **R:**7
  ancient, **R:**8-9
  in Africa, **R:**40-41
  in Asia, **R:**10-31
  in Europe and Americas, 32-39
  in Oceania and Polynesia, **R:**42-43
  See also Buddhism; Christianity; Confucianism; gods and goddesses; Hinduism; Islam; Jainism; Shinto; Sikhism; Taoism
reliquaries, **EL:**10
Remembrance Day, **EL:**32
Renaissance, **BG:**10, **EL:**10, **M:**7, 9
Rendille (people), **BG:**37
Resurrection, **S:**24, 30
Revere, Paul, **N:**30
Revolutionary War in America, **N:**7, 30-32
rice, **E:**41, **R:**13
  in birth and growing up celebrations, **BG:**16, 20, 21
  in harvest celebrations, **H:**13-19, 26
  in New Year celebrations, **NY:**14, 16, 19, 23
  in spring celebrations, **S:**13-15
  in weddings, **M:**21, 30
riddle-guessing, **S:**10
Rideau Canal, **W:**37
Ridvan (festival), **R:**31
Rig-Veda (text), **BG:**21
rings, **M:**16, 28
  Bahá'í, **R:**30
  engagement, **M:**9, 34
  wedding, **M:**9, 13, 21, 24, 30, 32, 34
Rinpoche, Guru, **S:**20
Rio de Janeiro (Brazil), **S:**27
rites of passage, **BG:**7
  See also coming of age; initiation rites
robes, deerskin, **BG:**34, 35
Roll of Honour Wall, **N:**43
rolls (food), **W:**29
Roma (people), **S:**34

Roman Catholic Church, **H:**34, **N:**22
  birth and growing up in, **BG:**10, 16, 30, 31
  funeral rites in, **EL:**11, 30, 31
  harvest celebrations in, **H:**10, 29, 38, 39
  marriage in, **M:**30, 32, 37
  New Year in, **NY:**39
  religious celebrations in, **R:**35, 37-39, 43
  spring celebrations in, **S:**14, 26-27
  winter celebrations in, **W:**30, 32
  See also Christianity
Romania, **N:**29, **S:**31
Roman Laughing Day, **S:**33
Rome (Italy), **N:**27, **S:**31
Rome, ancient
  birth and growing up in, **BG:**9
  Christianity in, **W:**26, 28
  everyday rituals in, **E:**7, 8, 29
  funeral rites in, **EL:**10
  harvest celebrations in, **H:**9
  marriage in, **M:**7, 9
  New Year in, **NY:**7, 8, 32
  religious celebrations in, **R:**9, 32
  spring celebrations in, **S:**8, 9, 32, 33
  winter celebrations in, **W:**8, 9
Romulus and Remus, **S:**32
Roosevelt, Theodore, **W:**35
roosters, **M:**11, 14
rosary, **EL:**30
Rosca de Reyes (cake), **W:**39
Rose Bowl, **NY:**36
Rose Festival, **S:**40
rosemary (plant), **N:**43
roses, **S:**33, 40
Rosh Ha-Shanah, **N:**20, **NY:**26-28
Ross, Betsy, **N:**32
Rot Naam Dam Hua (ceremony), **NY:**17
royal funerals, **EL:**31
Royal Plowing Festival, **H:**16
Rua (god), **W:**42
Rural Diónysia (festival), **W:**8
Russia, **H:**30-31, **N:**10, 28, **NY:**35

Russian Orthodox Church. *See* Eastern Orthodox Churches
Ruth, Book of, **H:**25
Ruwatan (ritual), **E:**17

S

Sabah (Malaysia), **H:**17
Sabbath, **E:**24, 25
sabzeh (greens), **S:**23
sacraments, **BG:**30-31, **M:**30
Sacred Thread ceremony, **BG:**21
sacred tooth of Buddha, **R:**17
sacrifice
  in everyday rituals, **E:**16, 19, 38
  in funeral rites, **EL:**10-11, 13, 14, 36, 38
  in harvest celebrations, **H:**8, 9, 11, 17, 19, 24
  in religious celebrations, **R:**10
  in spring celebrations, **S:**9, 11, 18, 22, 29
  in weddings, **M:**9
  in winter celebrations, **W:**9, 10, 16, 17
  See also animal sacrifice; human sacrifice
Sadeh (festival), **W:**24, 25
sadhus (holy men), **W:**19
Sagdid (ritual), **EL:**22, 25
St. Anthony of Padua, Festival of, **W:**39
St. Basil's Day, **NY:**7, 32-35
Saintes-Maries-de-la-Mer (France), **S:**34
St. John the Baptist, Festival of, **W:**39
St. Joseph's Day, **W:**7, 33
St. Lucia Day, **W:**28-29
St. Nicholas Day, **W:**7, 26-27
St. Patrick's Day, **W:**7, 32
St. Paul's Winter Carnival, **W:**36
St. Peter, Festival of, **W:**39
St. Peter's Basilica, **EL:**11, **NY:**34
St. Peter's Square (Rome), **S:**31
St. Valentine's Day, **S:**9, 32, 33

sake (beverage), **M:**13
salmon, **S:**7
salt, **E:**19, **M:**33
Samarqand (Uzbekistan), **M:**23
samba schools, **S:**27
Samhain (festival), **EL:**33, **N:**23, **NY:**9
Samil Movement, **N:**11
Samoa, **M:**43
Samoset, **H:**35
samskaras (ceremonies), **BG:**20-21, **EL:**20
samurai, **S:**12
Sana (people), **BG:**39
Sande (organization), **BG:**40
Sandeks (religious officials), **BG:**25
sand paintings, **E:**22, 35
Sanganichi (festival), **NY:**14
San Geremia, Church of, **W:**28
San Juan Chamula (church), **NY:**39
San Martin, José de, **N:**37
San Nicola, Basilica of, **W:**27
sans-culottes (soldiers), **N:**24
Santa Lucia Day, **W:**28
Sapporo Snow Festival, **W:**12
Sara, St., **S:**34
Saraswati (goddess), **S:**16
Saraswati Puja (festival), **S:**16
saris (garments), **M:**17
Sassanian dynasty, **W:**25
Saturn (god), **W:**9
Saturnalia (festival), **W:**9
Saudi Arabia, **EL:**26, **R:**26
  See also Mecca; Medina
saunas, **E:**28, 29
Scandinavia, ancient, **W:**9
scarification, **BG:**43
school. *See* education
school proms, **BG:**32, 33
scones, **E:**31
Scotland, **M:**31, **NY:**32, 33, **S:**33
sculptures, snow and ice, **W:**10-12, 36
seasons
  in Africa, **W:**8, 40
  in Asia, **W:**16, 24
  in Latin America, **W:**38
  in Oceania, **W:**42
  See also calendar

Sebae (ritual), **NY:**16
secret societies, **BG:**38, 40
sedan chairs, **M:**10
Seder, **N:**18, 20
Seijin-no-hi (holiday), **BG:**15
Sekaten Maulud (festival), **R:**13
Seleucid empire, **W:**21
Semana Santa (week), **S:**29
Senegal, **BG:**39, 41, **S:**38
Senufo (people), **BG:**41, **EL:**39-41
Seol (year), **NY:**16
Seollal (day), **NY:**16
Sephardic Jews, **BG:**24, 25
sepoys (soldiers), **N:**14
Septuagint (book), **W:**20
Serbia and Montenegro, **N:**29
Setsubun (festival), **S:**13
7-5-3 Festival, **BG:**14
Seven Symbols, **S:**23
Shabbat. *See* Sabbath
Shadi (festivity), **M:**22
shahada (ritual), **BG:**29
Shai (people), **BG:**40
Shalako (ceremony), **NY:**37
shamans, **BG:**35, **E:**36, **R:**38
shamash (candle), **W:**23
shamrock, **W:**32
Shapur I, **W:**25
Shavuot (festival), **H:**24-25
Sheb-i Arus (festival), **W:**24
sheep, **H:**28
Shema (prayer), **E:**24
shemu (season), **W:**8
Shennong (legend), **H:**13
shepherds, **R:**7, 32
Shiah Muslims, **NY:**30, 31
Shichi-go-San (festival), **BG:**14
shield, initiation, **BG:**38
Shi Huangdi, **EL:**8
Shinbyu ceremony, **BG:**17
Shinto, **H:**15, **W:**13
  birth and growing up in, **BG:**14-15
  everyday rituals in, **E:**14
  funeral rites in, **EL:**16
  marriage in, **M:**12, 13
  New Year in, **NY:**15
  religious celebrations in, **R:**12
  spring celebrations in, **S:**12, 13
ship burial, **EL:**11
Shiva (god), **M:**17, **R:**18, 20, 22, **S:**18, **W:**18
shiva (ritual), **EL:**28

shivaree (custom), **M:**37
shoes
  in birth and growing up celebrations, **BG:**10, 12, 15, 33
  in everyday rituals, **E:**15, 18, 21
  in winter celebrations, **W:**7, 12, 26, 27, 39
shofar, **NY:**26, 29
Shona (people), **EL:**39
Shrove Tuesday, **S:**26-28
Siam. *See* Thailand
siapo dresses, **M:**43
Sicily, **EL:**31, **W:**33
Siddartha Gautama. *See* Buddha
Sierra Leone, **BG:**40
Sikhism, **N:**17, **W:**16
  birth and growing up in, **BG:**22-23
  everyday rituals in, **E:**21
  harvest celebrations in, **H:**21
  marriage in, **M:**20
  New Year in, **NY:**7, 20
  religious celebrations in, **R:**23
Simeon (Biblical figure), **R:**33
simhat bat (ritual), **BG:**25
Singapore, **H:**13, **N:**12, **NY:**12
singing. *See* music
Sinterklaas, **W:**27
Sioux Indians, **BG:**7
sitting in state, **M:**15
Siyyid 'Alí Muhammad. *See* Báb
skeletons, **EL:**7, 36
skulls, **EL:**24, 36
  buffalo, **BG:**35, **R:**37
sky burial, **EL:**7, 25
Sky Woman (goddess), **R:**36
slavery
  in Africa, **NY:**41
  in Latin America, **N:**37, **NY:**39, **S:**27
  in Rome, **W:**9
  in United States, **M:**36, **N:**7, 34, **W:**35
  Jewish, **N:**18-20
sledding, **W:**36, 37
Slovakia, **M:**33, **N:**28, **W:**27
Slovenia, **N:**29
Smith, Joseph, **R:**35
snake-boat races, **H:**20
Snake Ceremony, **H:**33

Cumulative Index

sneezing, **E:**29
snowmen, **W:**12
snowshoes, **W:**7
Solar New Year, **NY:**7
Solidarity (union), **N:**29
Solomon Islands, **M:**43
solstice, summer, **H:**11
solstice, winter, **H:**10, 11
    in New Year celebrations, **NY:**10, 33, 34, 43
    in winter celebrations, **W:**8, 10, 24, 42
Somalia, **M:**7
Songkran (festival), **NY:**17
songpyon (cakes), **H:**15
soup, **BG:**29, **W:**10, 12
sourvakari (ceremony), **NY:**35
South Africa, **BG:**41, **E:**40, **M:**40, **N:**39-41
South America. *See* Latin America
Southern Hemisphere, **W:**7
Soviet Union, **H:**31, **N:**28
Spain, **BG:**25, **S:**35, 43, **W:**27
    as colonial power, **H:**39, **N:**13, 36-38
    everyday rituals in, **E:**9, 30
    marriage in, **M:**31
    mourning in, **EL:**31
    New Year in, **NY:**33
    spring celebrations in, **S:**29
    winter celebrations in, **W:**30, 33
spas, **E:**29
Spenta Mainyu (spirit), **EL:**22
spirits. *See* afterlife beliefs; gods and goddesses
sports
    in everyday rituals, **E:**8, 33
    in harvest celebrations, **H:**11, 20, 36, 42
    in marriage celebrations, **M:**23, 27
    in New Year celebrations, **NY:**15, 36, 37
    in religious celebrations, **R:**8, 41, 43
    in winter celebrations, **W:**11, 36, 37, 40
    See also games
spring, **NY:**7, 11

spring celebrations, **S:**7
    in Africa, **S:**38-41
    in Americas, **S:**7, 36-37
    in ancient world, **S:**8-9
    in Asia, **S:**10-25
    in Australasia and Oceania, **S:**42-43
    in Europe, **S:**7-9, 26-35
Spring Festival, **NY:**7, 10-13
Squanto, **H:**35
Sri Lanka, **E:**23, **R:**7, 16, 17, 23
stamps, **N:**8, 11, 39
Standish, Miles, **H:**34
"Star-Spangled Banner, The," **N:**32
Statue of Liberty, **N:**32
stick dance, **R:**21
stilt walkers, **R:**41
stocking (project), **W:**31
stone laying (ritual), **EL:**29
Stowe, Harriet Beecher, **N:**34
stupas (shrines), **R:**16
Sucre, Antonio José de, **N:**37
Sudan, **EL:**38, **M:**27
Sufism, **E:**27, **W:**24
Suharto, **N:**13
suicide, **EL:**21
Sukarno, **N:**13
sukkah (shelters), **H:**22, 23
Sukkot (festival), **H:**22-23
Sukra (god), **M:**17
Sumerians, **EL:**8, **NY:**8
sun, **H:**10, 18, 32, **R:**9
sun dance, **R:**37
Sun Festival, **H:**10
Sunni Muslims, **NY:**30
Sunrise Ceremony, **BG:**35
superstition, **E:**28, 29
Suri Festival, **S:**23
Surma (people), **EL:**38
Surya (god), **H:**18
suttee (ritual), **EL:**21
Swahili (people), **NY:**41
Swaziland, **H:**41, **M:**40
sweat lodges, **E:**35
Sweden, **E:**30, **M:**35, **W:**28, 29
swimming, **NY:**37
    winter, **W:**11
Switzerland, **H:**28, **NY:**32, 33
swords, **BG:**38, **S:**41
Sybylline (text), **E:**9
Sydney (Australia), **N:**43, **NY:**42

sympathy cards, **EL:**16, 35
synagogues, **BG:**24, 26, 27, **E:**24, 25, **H:**23, **M:**24, **N:**20, **W:**22
Syria, **M:**29, **S:**25

T

Tablets of the Law, **BG:**27
tabots (boxes), **W:**41
Tahiti, **M:**43
Tahnik (ritual), **BG:**28
tái chi, **E:**11
Taiwan, **EL:**15, **H:**13
Tajikistan, **M:**22
tako-age (entertainment), **NY:**15
tallits (garments), **BG:**26, **E:**25
Talmud, **NY:**26, 29, **W:**21
Tamils (people), **R:**43
Tam Kung (god), **R:**11
Taneka (people), **BG:**39
tangerines, **NY:**12
tangihangas (rituals), **EL:**42
tang yuan (soup), **W:**10
ta no kami (god), **H:**15
Taoism, **E:**11, 13, **EL:**12, 18, **R:**10, 11, **S:**11
Tashlikh (ritual), **NY:**28
tatanua masks, **EL:**43
tazias (symbols), **NY:**31
tea, **E:**7, 10, 14, 30, 31, 36, **M:**11
Tea Act, **N:**30
tefillins (boxes), **BG:**26
television, **E:**33
Temple, in Jerusalem, **R:**33, **W:**20-23
temples
    Buddhist, **S:**20
    Hindu, **S:**16, 17
    Jain, **EL:**23
    Parsi, **EL:**22
Ten Commandments, **BG:**27, **H:**24, **W:**41
Ten Days of Penitence, **NY:**26
Tendis (gatherings), **M:**39
Tenochtitlan (city), **R:**9
Tet Festival, **S:**15
Tet Trung Thu (festival), **H:**14

Texas, **N:**7, 34, 35
thaalis (necklaces), **M:**19
Thai (month), **H:**19
Thailand
    birth and growing up in, **BG:**18-19
    everyday rituals in, **E:**12, 13, 16, 17, 22, 23
    funeral rites in, **EL:**18, 19
    harvest celebrations in, **H:**16
    marriage in, **M:**14
    national celebrations in, **N:**12
    New Year in, **NY:**17-19
    spring in, **S:**14
Thalysia (festival), **H:**9
thangkas (paintings), **E:**23, **S:**20
Thanksgiving Day
    American, **H:**7, 34-37
    Canadian, **H:**7, 35
    German, **H:**28
theater, **E:**17, **EL:**14
Thesmophoria (festival), **H:**9
Thor (god), **W:**9
Three Kings Day. *See* Epiphany
Three Sisters (goddesses), **H:**32
Three Wise Men, **W:**30, 31, 39
Tibet, **M:**22, **N:**8, **NY:**18, **R:**23, **S:**20
    everyday rituals in, **E:**7, 9, 12, 22-23
    funeral rites in, **EL:**24-25
    New Year in, **NY:**7, 24-25
tikas (marks), **M:**17
tikis (pendants), **E:**43
Tilak, Bal G., **N:**15
Times Square (New York City), **NY:**37
Timkat (festival), **W:**41
Timucua Indians, **S:**36
Tirthankaras (spirits), **EL:**23
tish (ritual), **M:**25
Tislet (legend), **M:**39
Tiwi Islands, **EL:**43, **R:**43
toe-rings, **M:**16
Togo, **NY:**40, 41
togu nas (houses), **E:**38
Tomb of the Unknown Soldier, **EL:**34, 35
tombs. *See* burial
Tomb Sweeping Day, **S:**11
Tonga, **M:**43
tooth filing, **M:**15

Torah, **BG:**26, 27, **H:**24, 25, **N:**19, **NY:**26, 28, **W:**20

tormas (food), **NY:**24

tortoise play, **H:**15

Toshikoshi (ritual), **NY:**14

totem poles, **EL:**34

totems (spirits), **M:**42

Tournament of Roses Parade, **NY:**36

Tower of Silence, **EL:**7, 22

trances, **R:**40

trickery, **S:**19, 22, 23, 33

Trinity, **BG:**30

Trobriand Islands, **M:**43

Tsagaan Sar (festival), **W:**14-15

tsampa (food), **NY:**25

Tuareg (people), **M:**39

Tu B'Shevat (holiday), **NY:**29

tulips, **S:**43

turban-tying ceremony, **BG:**23

Turkana doll, **BG:**36

Turkey, **M:**29, **N:**43, **NY:**31, **S:**25, **W:**24

turkey (food), **H:**34, 36, **R:**34

Turkmenistan, **N:**28

Tutu, Desmond, **N:**40

twins, **BG:**37

Tzotzil (people), **NY:**39

U

Uganda, **EL:**38

Ujjain (India), **W:**19

Ukraine, **BG:**32, **H:**31, **M:**33, **N:**28, **NY:**35

umbrellas, **M:**13

Umhlanga (festival), **M:**40

Uncle Tom's Cabin (Stowe), **N:**34

unction (ritual), **EL:**30

United Kingdom
  as colonial power, **N:**9, 12, 14-15, 30-32, 38, 40
  Guy Fawkes Day in, **N:**22-23
  harvest celebrations in, **H:**26-27
  royal funeral in, **EL:**31
  spring celebrations in, **S:**8, 9, 33-35
  See also England

United Nations, **N:**8, 21

United States, **M:**29, **N:**10, 13
  birth and growing up in, **BG:**7, 32-35
  everyday rituals in, **E:**32-35
  harvest celebrations in, **H:**7, 32-38
  independence of, **N:**7, 30-35
  marriage in, **M:**34-37
  New Year in, **NY:**36-37
  religious celebrations in, **R:**34-37
  spring celebrations in, **S:**34-37
  winter celebrations in, **W:**7, 28, 32, 34-36
  See also Indians, American

Upanayana samskara (ceremony), **BG:**21

Ur (city), **EL:**8

Uruguay, **E:**36

Ute Indians, **S:**37

Uzbekistan, **M:**22, 23, **N:**28, 29

V

Vaisakh (festival), **H:**21

Valencia (Spain), **W:**33

Valentine, St., **S:**32

Valentine's Day, **S:**32, 33

Valima (festivity), **M:**22

Vamana (god), **R:**19

Vanuatu Islands, **H:**43

Varaha (god), **R:**19

Varalakshmi (deity), **M:**18

Varanasi (India), **EL:**21

Vardhamana Mahavira, **E:**20

Vasant Panchami (festival), **S:**16-17

Vasilopitta (cake), **NY:**33-35

Vatican City, **NY:**34

vegetables (recipe), **EL:**15

vegetarianism, **E:**19-21

veils, **M:**25, 27, 33, 38

Venezuela, **H:**39, **N:**37, **NY:**38, 39

Venice (Italy), **EL:**32, **S:**26

Vesta (goddess), **E:**8

Vestal Virgins, **E:**8

Viareggio (Italy), **S:**26

Victor Emmanuel II of Italy, **N:**27

Victoria, queen of United Kingdom, **EL:**31, **M:**30, **N:**15

Vidyarambha samskara (ceremony), **BG:**21

Vienna (Austria), **NY:**34

Vietnam, **EL:**18, **H:**14, **R:**14, **S:**7, 14, 15

Vietnam Veterans Memorial, **EL:**35

Vikings, **BG:**9, **EL:**11, **NY:**32, **W:**9

Vishnu (god), **BG:**20, **H:**20, **M:**18, **NY:**22, **R:**18, 19, **S:**18, **W:**18

Vishu (festival), **S:**16, 17

vishu-kani, **S:**17

Vision Quest (ceremony), **BG:**35

Voladores, Dance of the, **H:**39

Volos (god), **H:**31

voodoo, **R:**40

voting, **BG:**32, 33, **N:**41

Voyageur Festival, **W:**37

vultures, **EL:**22, 25

W

Wailing Wall. *See* Western Wall

Waitangi, Treaty of, **N:**42

Waitangi Day, **N:**42

wakes, **EL:**30

Walesa, Lech, **N:**29

waltz, **NY:**34

Wampanoag Indians, **H:**35

war bonnets, **E:**34

warrior status, **BG:**38

Warsaw Ghetto Uprising, **EL:**29

washing, **E:**19, 26, 27, 41, **H:**23, **M:**18
  See also bathing; purification rituals

Washington, D.C., **EL:**35

Washington, George, **H:**35, **N:**31, 32, **W:**35

water lanterns, **EL:**15

watermelons, **W:**25

water rituals
  birth and growing up, **BG:**9, 16, 30
  New Year, **NY:**17, 19, 24, 37
  winter, **W:**11-13, 18-19, 41
  See also bathing; washing

Wayang Kulit (play), **E:**17

weaving, **E:**37

weddings, **M:**7
  carrying of bride, **M:**10, 37
  in Africa, **M:**38-41
  in Americas, **M:**34-37
  in Asia, **M:**10-29
  in Europe, **M:**30-33
  in history, **M:**8-9
  in Pacific, **M:**42-43
  processions, **M:**8, 14, 29, 39
  unveiling of bride, **M:**33

Weeks, Feast of.
  See Shavuot

weilu (feast), **NY:**12

Wesak (festival), **R:**13-15

Western Wall (Jerusalem), **BG:**26, **E:**24, 25, **H:**23, 24, **W:**21

wheat, **H:**8, 9, 24, 27, 29

Wheel of Dharma, **E:**23

Whiro (god), **EL:**42

white (color), **EL:**13

White Month.
  See Tsagaan Sar

White-Painted Woman (goddess), **BG:**35

whites
  South African, **N:**40-41
  United States, **N:**35

wicker men (effigies), **N:**23

wine
  in birth and growing up celebrations, **BG:**27, 31
  in harvest celebrations, **H:**23, 26
  in New Year celebrations, **NY:**27, 28, 34
  in Seder, **N:**20
  in wedding ceremonies, **M:**13, 25, 32, 33

Winnipeg (Manitoba), **W:**37

winter celebrations, **W:**7
  in Africa, **W:**40-41
  in Americas, **W:**34-39
  in ancient world, **W:**8-9
  in Asia, **W:**10-25
  in Europe, **W:**26-33
  in Oceania, **W:**42-43

Winterlude festival, **W:**37

witches, **EL:**33

women
  in ancient Rome, **M:**9
  in end-of-life rituals, **EL:**21, 27, 31
  Islam and, **E:**26, 27, **M:**26

Woodson, Carter G., **W:**35

work prohibitions, **NY:**27

Cumulative Index

World War I, **EL:**32, **M:**29, **N:**43

World War II, **EL:**29, **N:**10, 27

wreaths, **H:**28, 30, 31, **R:**32

X

Xilonen (goddess), **H:**9

Xochiquetzal (goddess), **S:**8

Y

yaake (dance), **M:**38

yachting, **R:**43

Yahrzeit candles, **NY:**29

Yalda (festival), **W:**24, 25

Yama (god), **EL:**20, **NY:**22, 23

yam-no-kami (god), **R:**12

yam paintings, **E:**37

yams, **H:**40, 42, 43, **NY:**7, 40

Yanomami Indians, **H:**38, 39, **N:**8

Yap (island), **N:**9

yarmulkas (caps), **BG:**26, **E:**24, 25, **NY:**29

yawulyu (ritual), **BG:**42

Yaya Matsuri (festival), **W:**13

Yazid, **NY:**30, 31

yellow (color), **S:**16, 21

Yemen, **M:**28

Yena (spirit), **H:**43

Yi (people), **E:**13

yin and yang, **E:**11, **H:**12, **N:**10, **W:**10

yoga, **E:**11, 19

Yom Hashoah (holiday), **EL:**29

Yomi (myth), **EL:**10

Yom Kippur, **N:**20, **NY:**26, 28

Yorktown (Virginia), **N:**31

Yoruba (people), **BG:**36, 38, **E:**39, **EL:**39, **H:**40, **NY:**40

Yugoslavia, **N:**29

Yu Huang Shang-ti.
    See Jade emperor

yui-no status, **M:**12

Yule (feast), **W:**9

yurts. *See* ger

Yut (game), **NY:**16

Z

Zamzam, well of, **R:**27

Zapotec Indians, **H:**9

Zen Buddhism, **E:**14

Zeus (god), **W:**21

zeved habat (ceremony), **BG:**25

Zhang Zhongjing, **W:**10

Zhong Qiu (festival), **H:**12-13

Zhuazhou ceremony, **BG:**12

Zimbabwe, **EL:**39

Zionism, **N:**21

zodiac, **E:**29

Zoroaster, **EL:**22, **H:**11, **R:**30, **S:**22

Zoroastrianism
    end-of-life rituals in, **EL:**22
    harvest celebrations in, **H:**11
    New Year in, **NY:**7
    spring celebrations in, **S:**22, 23
    winter celebrations in, **W:**24-25

Zuhak, King, **S:**25

Zulu (people), **M:**40, **N:**41

Zuni (people), **NY:**37

zurnas (instruments), **M:**29